I0411643

40 Weeks
Happily Ever After

Kelly Brake

All scripture quotations, unless otherwise indicated, are taken from the
New King James Version®.

Copyright © 1982 by Thomas Nelson, Inc. Used by permission. All rights reserved.

Copyright © 2015 Robert K. Brake

All rights reserved.

ISBN: 1508860033
ISBN-13:9781508860037

DEDICATION

I have not mastered the craft of married life, but largely due to my amazing wife and best friend, I have learned much over the years. This life learning experience, has enabled us both to enjoy our journey at a level we had not known possible, when we first exchanged our own vows. No one therefore, could be more deserving of this book's dedication than the one who has been the most enduring, most faith-filled, and most extraordinary life partner a man could ever dream of having, my beautiful wife Lenora.

CONTENTS

Author's Introduction

Forty weeks before the wedding of my son Jonathan, to his fiancé Lynn, I was praying about what I could do to bless them in a unique way. It came to me in a flash, and I immediately knew it was an inspiration from the heart of God. I was to take the accumulated experiences and lessons that I had walked through and learned with my own bride, Lenora, of over 30 years, and condense these into a 40 week marriage devotional. I would write, one devotional every Friday for the 40 weeks leading up to their special day. It would be my private and very personal gift to them, for their eyes only, or so I thought.

Upon completion, more than one family member began to appeal that I make these devotionals available to a wider audience. After much thought, and with Jonny & Lynn's permission, the decision was made. So, with only a few minor editorial adjustments to eliminate some lines (that were comprehensible to family only,) the process of putting this into print was begun.

I decided to leave these devotionals 99% intact, exactly as they were written, as heart felt thoughts from a father to his children. The humor that we use in our family, the style of writing that I use with my children and friends, these have been left unaltered. The result is a very non-typical marriage devotional, but then, it was the intent from the beginning to provide for my son and his bride something unique and non-typical.

Though written with two young people in mind, I do believe that God's principles are timeless and can be valuable to all. Whether you are newlywed, midway through life's journey, or in the latter years of a long and faithful covenant, there is something in these pages that can stir us all.

- *Kelly Brake*

WEEK #1
JESUS: THE KEY TO EVERYTHING

What makes a marriage last? What makes marriage happy, fulfilling, desirable, and fun? The world pays big bucks to find solutions to the crises in their homes. They travel to seminars, sit in long sessions with counselors, watch videos, and read self-help books. While these are all well and good, there is one simple ingredient that surpasses all others in securing our lives together as husbands and wives: it is the person of Jesus. He is the Savior at the center of our life and home. He is the glue, the counselor, the revealer of all we need to make this challenge of married life work with excellence.

Our pursuit of Jesus must surpass all other goals. When a home is governed by a man and woman who mutually share the priority of a relationship with God, that home is unstoppable. Jesus is never stagnant or uninteresting. Jesus stimulates our thoughts, emotions and passions. When Jesus is Lord...when we pursue Him mutually with all of our hearts... then our bond becomes unbreakable.

Because He is alive and breathes life, the home that pursues Him stays alive and filled with the breath of God. Discord and discontentment are not inevitable, however. Peace can predominate, because the Prince of Peace is allowed to remain in His rightful place. When He is our first love, our love for one another continues to burn and even intensify. Jesus, who most perfectly exhibits love, teaches us how to love one another. Jesus, the ultimate servant, grants us joy in serving. Jesus, who gave the supreme sacrifice, helps us to be givers and continually lay down our lives. He who denied Himself leads us into the wonderful freedom of living for one another.

Jesus...He is the key to everything in marriage. When a man and woman love Jesus above all else, even above one another, they have created a place for the glory of God to dwell! Their children will grow up in peace. Their table will be abundant and their cup will run over.

While others grow bored and weary of this life, their eyes will burn brightly with an ever increasing revelation of the greatness of God. With each passing year, the joy of covenant will intensify, and their gratitude for His faithfulness will form a bond between them that the world cannot comprehend. Jesus...He makes it work...He makes it wonderful...He makes all things beautiful in His perfect time.

The marriage covenant is a weighty decision, but fear not! For *"He who began a good work in you, will bring it to completion and fulfill it until the day of Jesus Christ." (Philippians 1:6)* Not only will He complete us and fulfill us, but in Acts 17:28 it says *"For in Him we live, and move, and have our being."* Furthermore, Colossians 1:17 says *"And He is before all things, and in Him all things are held together."*

With God first in our lives, we have His promise that He will personally oversee our marriage until the day of Jesus Christ.

WEEK #2
LAUGHING YOUR WAY TO A HAPPY HOME

People do all sorts of crazy things to get the endorphins moving in their bodies. When endorphins are released, the brain tells the rest of the body that "all is well!" God designed these sensory stimulators to enable us to feel wonderful and happy, which is exactly how He wants His kids to feel. Without God, folks resort to doing whatever they can to keep those endorphins releasing into the brain: drugs, alcohol, food, entertainment, extreme sports and excessive exercise. Things that are both good and bad are pursued to find that sense of euphoria and continue the endorphin high.

The majority of marriages grow stale way sooner than the blissful newlyweds ever imagined. However, some homes seem able to stay "alive and well" for years beyond the norm. What makes the difference? Numerous couples were interviewed that have been happily married for 50, 60, and even 70+ years, and all had one common denominator: they learned how to laugh.

Some entered marriage with this already entrenched in their personalities, but most had to learn it. And in learning to laugh, many saved not only their marriage, but even their very lives.

Laughter has stilled the storm, brought them back from the brink, comforted their loved ones, and brightened their future. Laughter became for them an outlet, a dissipater of conflict, a pathway to unity, and a navigator through confusion. It built their faith, healed their bodies, took away their fears, and even dried their tears.

The religious find excess laughter to be inappropriate...the domain of children and the simple minded. But was it not Jesus Himself who said that "unless we become like little children, we cannot enter the kingdom of heaven"? To know the fullness of our Father's house, a childlike freedom from judgment and disapproval must be cultivated all of our days. A child knows when he is in a home that loves children! He isn't shushed, he isn't in the way, and he isn't constantly in danger of incurring the wrath of the homeowner by shattering their beloved valuables. The home is child friendly.

A husband and wife have a responsibility to cultivate a child friendly home; not for the children they *will* parent, but rather for the child that must be preserved within each of their own hearts. Doing this will create a home where there is no fear of failure or rejection for imperfection; a home where you can laugh off your mistakes and accept your own humanity; a home where you can laugh at yourselves and with one another.

Be purposeful in releasing endorphins into your marriage! The Holy Spirit is the world's finest humorist. He will show you the lighter side of life! And remember, when all in this world seems dark and heading in the wrong direction, Psalm 2:4 tells us that *"The Lord sits in the heavens and **laughs**!"*

Proverbs 17:22 "A MERRY HEART DOES GOOD, LIKE MEDICINE!"

WEEK #3
"MANGIA"

Ah, one of the greatest words in the Italian language..... "mangia"!
It simply means to "eat up" or "enjoy the feast set before you".
And herein lies one of the great secrets of a happy home: FOOD!

Sounds utterly carnal, but in fact, the Bible has a great deal to say
about food, family meals, and the wonderful fellowship that can
be enjoyed around the "core life" activity of eating. Now, first of
all, let's dispense with the philosophical nonsense espoused by
some that "they only eat to survive" and "we really aren't into
it....it's just a biological necessity". Well, we've met a few of these
espousers of misery, and be assured they are totally off the wall
on this subject. It would be like saying that sex is only for having
babies... something we do for the survival of the species. What a
strange view of life, and what a strange view of God.

For in fact, God designed us as sensory beings not simply for
species perpetuation and personal survival, but also for the
enjoyment of those things He has created. He is a Father that
delights in delighting His children! And thus the pleasure of taste,
not solely for the purpose of avoiding the rancid and rotten, but
also for the savoring of the succulent and sweet.

Food is meant to be a pleasure. The centering of a family's life together around an aromatic and well prepared table builds tradition, stimulates interaction, and promotes joy. Special days and holidays are marked by treats and tasty morsels that have been passed down from generations.

God loves a good celebration! In the Old Testament there was even an occasion when the gathered tithes of the people of Israel were to be utilized for a massive national feasting party. When they marked special observances of God's faithfulness, they did so with special foods and everyone got involved in the preparation process. We also find in the Old Testament times when men were cooking (Jacob), angels were cooking (cakes for Elijah), God was cooking (fire coming down upon the sacrifices of the altar), and once in a while, even the ladies would have a turn in the kitchen!

Meals are an equal opportunity adventure. Creativity, experimentation, trial and error all become part of the journey toward shared family experience and the reward for success is enjoyed by all. Memories are created. Children discover God as provider through the abundance of the table, and God as nurturer through the efforts put into making something that will put a smile on their faces and a warmth in their bellies.

One of the greatest benefits of family meal time is the opportunity for bonding and conversation between parents and children. Guard your times around the table! Banish electronic disruption, and opt instead for a protected hour where the TV and telephones are muted, and everyone knows that only the most serious of emergencies will break into these treasured family moments.

Let's consider a few thoughts from the book of Nehemiah. There had been a rediscovering of the Law, long lost while the people of Israel were in exile. With a reading of the law, they all realized how badly they had missed the mark. So, we would be inclined to think they were due for a long season of sorrow and fasting, right? But we would be quite wrong. In fact, it was the opposite. Ezra the priest told them all to stop crying, go home, and "start preparing something delicious to eat!"

"Go your way, eat the fat, drink the sweet, and send portions to those for whom nothing is prepared; for this day is holy to our Lord. Do not sorrow, for the joy of the Lord is your strength! And all the people went their way to eat and drink, to send portions and rejoice greatly, because they understood the words that were declared to them." (Nehemiah 8:10,12)

Wow... God is definitely into making sure that we enjoy this world He created! If we truly *"understood the words"* we would realize that real Christianity brings freedom to enjoy every part of life to the fullest! We would know that spirituality is not summarized in self-mortification and ritualistic denial, but in a passionate celebration of our forgiveness, and our position as sons and daughters of God.

So... ***mangia***! Enjoy your blessings and fill your home with life and celebration around the kitchen and table. Eat well, eat healthy, and give thanks daily for the amazing God who makes sure that His children are never begging for bread; they have a table spread before them in the presence of their enemies, and they have a cup that forever is running over!

"You shall eat in plenty and be satisfied, and praise the name of the Lord your God, who has dealt wondrously with you; and My people shall never be put to shame." Joel 2:26

WEEK #4
WHO NEEDS MONEY WHEN
YOU CAN LIVE ON LOVE!

What a lovely sounding romantic theory. But the problem is that it doesn't work, except in poetry and love songs. In real life money is a necessity, and the lack of it is a challenge that has won the title of "most common cause of marital frustration and/or termination". This being the case, every husband and wife ought to make "basic agreement on the purpose, use, and role of money in our home" as a top level goal. It should be restudied year by year as money comes and goes (and comes and goes) sometimes going faster than it is coming! With good management and Biblical principles, however, that does not have to be the case. God has designed a system that works in any economy, and in any nation for His people to have provision and even abundance.

Agreement in some key areas such as giving, cost of living, or borrowing will keep discord far away from the peace and sanctity of your castle. Since the acquisition of money usually involves hard work and/or sacrifice, people have super strong feelings about its misuse, loss, theft, or waste. No matter how pleasant a person you may be, if someone you love wastes what you've labored or believed for, it can be a painful breach to repair.

So here is a flat out, fail safe #1 principle when it comes to money: **Make generosity and a giving spirit the top financial safeguard in your home!** Agree together to be generous as a couple, and agree to allow one another to be individually generous. Be both faithful *and* generous with God, remembering that 10% of all your increase and profit belongs to Him. That is your faithfulness. Our generosity is found in the offerings we extend to support His work, His people, His mission, and His heart for the Kingdom of God, for the local church, for the gospel, and for the poor.

Don't fight over where the money goes, but make sure that it goes somewhere! When we follow the Divine example of generosity, we will always have the guarantee of an edge in what is an extremely competitive world. Opportunities come to us supernaturally. Job satisfaction becomes a fact, not a fantasy. Doors are opened, and God's favor follows us wherever we go.

Who in the world wouldn't want to live like that? Apparently, the great majority of people, and unfortunately even Christians. Statistics show that a very small number give even 10% in their tithe, let alone being generous above that standard. It is no wonder that so many find themselves drowning in debt and squabbling over every penny. That is no way to live, and it is not what God intended for His people.

Here are a few key principles that will help you to maintain a "giving lifestyle" for the long run and not just in moments of emotion or celebration:

1. Let God know that all you have is a resource for His use and direction. So many are afraid to do this, thinking God will drain their accounts. Not at all! God isn't interested in draining us (or fleecing us - that's what corrupt shepherds do). God is interested in blessing us, and blessing us in a big way. And often His means of blessing us is to grant us the privilege of

blessing others. "Those who sow generously will reap generously."

2. Keep record of your giving, and evaluate every few months what you are doing for others or for the kingdom of God. It is so easy for our money to start going more and more toward our own dreams and desires, but it is healthy to keep watch on ourselves to make sure that this discipline is functioning in a joyful way in our life. The Bible tells us to "check out our own hearts, to see whether we are indeed living a life of faith".

3. Giving takes a heart of faith, so if your faith walk and relationship with God is weak or untended, it will be extremely difficult for you to obey His promptings regarding giving. Your gut reaction to giving is a good barometer of where you are spiritually.

4. Hospitality in the home is an awesome form of giving. Making meals or providing a place to sleep for a family member or friend is a great type of ministry that we can work on together (because it usually takes both of us to clean the house up when company is coming!). Hospitality is hard work and it usually leaves everyone physically exhausted, but it is a great way to bless others and live out a giving lifestyle.

5. Make big giving decisions together, but allow one another the flexibility to give spontaneously on a smaller scale.

A truly spiritual marriage is the ultimate act of generosity - for both husband and wife will find themselves required to give completely, continuously, and sacrificially in order to carry out the mandate of Christ. In truth, a generous spirit will improve just about every aspect of our life and relationship.

Selfishness is at the root of most marital disunity, and how wonderful to get the upper hand over our own hoarding tendencies, and to find the true freedom that comes from emptying ourselves totally for the life of another. Be lavish with your time, your strength, your emotions, and your affection. "Give, and it shall be given unto you".

Philippians 2:5-7 "Let this mind be in you which was also in Christ Jesus, who being in the form of God, did not consider that position of privilege and equality something to be held on tightly to; but He emptied Himself of all reputation and advantage, and came in the likeness of men..."

II Corinthians 9:7-8 "So let each one give as he purposes in his own heart, not with resentment or out of obligation, for God loves a cheerful giver. And God is able to make all grace overflow to you, so that you always have enough in every area of life, and that you even have more than enough for the purpose of doing good works."

WEEK #5
MEN ARE FROM DIRT
WOMEN ARE FROM THE DIRT MAN'S RIB

This will be the "least romantic sounding title" of any devotional in this series. I like it because it sounds more original than "Men are from Mars - Women are from Venus". Plus it compels one to read further to investigate the eccentricity of the author.

But strangely, it is all Biblical. The Scriptures make it pointedly clear that humankind's genders were created each in a unique fashion: man (Adam) was made from the dust of the earth, and woman (Eve) was made from the rib bone of her husband. Totally weird, actually. But God has a purpose in everything He does.

"And the Lord God formed man out of the dust of the ground, and breathed into his nostrils the breath of life; and man became a living being. And the Lord God caused a deep sleep to fall on Adam, and he slept; and He took one of his ribs, and closed up the flesh in its place. Then the rib which the Lord God had taken from man He made into a woman, and He brought her to the man." Genesis 2:7 & 21-22

No wonder then that boys tend to get muddier and play rougher than girls... they are genetically predisposed to attract clouds of dust! And pity poor Eve. Ever since she came on the scene by diminishing the content of Adam's insides, he and his male descendants have been demanding hot food on the table after a long day at work to compensate for their handicapped bellies!

And men, when they get sick? Forget about it! After that first surgical procedure in the garden they've had a way lower pain tolerance than the ladies. Rib stealers beware... your man will forever expect you to atone for your theft by nursing his wounds with an extra measure of pity and pampering!

Okay, none of that is good theology. But men and women are different. We live in a 21st century secular world that works overtime to eliminate the uniqueness of male and female. But God has made the genders unique. Embrace that in one another, and it will be far easier to adjust to married life. If I demand that my wonderfully female wife adapt to my male particularities, well that is a pressure none can endure with a genuine smile on their face.

We so much want our spouse to be as we are. We want them to think the same way we think, to have the same emotional responses, and to communicate in the ways with which we are comfortable. It is a self-centered way of living, and it will strangle the beauty of our partner's unique creative identity before God. How much better to find ways to embrace and honor what God has created?

When differences surface in thinking and emotion, let us learn to celebrate the wisdom of God. There is a beautiful balance that comes to a family, and in particular to children, when men embrace their masculinity and women embrace their femininity. There is a wholeness and a maturity that comes to our decision making processes and our ability to handle the transitions of life. Less mistakes are made when a husband and wife are combining their unique makeup, and together are asking in humility for the guidance of the Lord. If all decisions are based solely on the husband's way of thinking, the error rate will increase. Likewise, the same will occur if the wife can only have it her way.

When "his way" and "her way" are combined into a mutual seeking of "God's way", a wonderful path unfolds before us and we discover that God really did know exactly what He was doing on that creation morning. It wasn't an experiment or a prototype.

Adam and Eve were wonderfully created, in the image of their Creator. Both of them infused with a variety of His distinctive attributes, but neither of them being an exact representation... that would be the privilege of His Son, Jesus Christ, who later would come to Earth in the flesh. But, a husband and wife in unity, together as two distinctly created people, are the closest picture this world can get outside of Jesus, of the amazing love, creative power, emotional intensity, and intellectual capacity of their Heavenly Father.

With my rib-mate, I am more effective at revealing the Gospel than on my own. In isolation, I tend to be preoccupied with the dust from which I came. But, when I behold my partner, taken historically from the side of my ancestor, I see our created co-dependence and our unbreakable bond. She came from man's side, then all men who followed came from her womb. We are completely different yet completely intertwined. Our destiny is linked to our diversity.

So seek wisdom for your marital journey from the ONLY one who totally understands both male and female; the God who created them. He knows how each one ticks. He knows their strengths and weaknesses. He will grant abundant wisdom, to not only gain insight into the mysterious brain of your spouse, but He will also grant grace to embrace those mysteries as they unfold in the years ahead.

"For this reason a man shall leave his father and mother and be joined to his wife, and the two shall become one flesh. This is a great mystery." Ephesians 5: 31-32

.

WEEK #6
COFFEE

They say that "Breakfast is the most important meal of the day". But I've learned that it is actually coffee! Twenty-five years without drinking it at all, and then one day the skies parted and I realized what an unfriendly husband I had been, leaving my dear wife to imbibe solo over all of those years. I repented, and with absolutely no affection or allegiance to the beverage, began intentionally to drink coffee first thing every morning. It transformed our travel life, as we now had a shared stimulant to begin our day, inspire our digestion, and free up our fuzzy brains. Not that my brain is fuzzy in the mornings, but now, after three years of drinking coffee daily, I've tricked my brain into believing that I cannot have a functional day without it. I am willingly enslaved.

It makes a huge difference how we start our day. Sharing a cup of coffee has actually accomplished its original intent, which was to find common ground well before the sun rises. We are on the same page now, and the intimacy is sweet!

How will you begin your day? Will it be to first turn on the television, check social media updates, respond to email or mobile messages, or run out the door late for work with a cup of coffee balanced in your hand? Will your day begin frantic or with peace? Will the world invade before you've barely opened your eyes, or will a moment be carved out for God's peace to invade your soul and build a fortress of resistance that can withstand anything the world may throw at you over the coming twelve hours?

You see, coffee is more than a beverage: it is a quiet shared moment, a chance for reflection, an opportunity for whispered thanksgiving to the Creator for His faithfulness through the night and His granting of the privilege of another day. It is a time to talk about shared dreams and desires. A marriage moment that belongs to the two of you alone. The day will begin soon enough, and the world's demands will press in. Noise, appointments, and obligations will cascade down upon you one after the other. Can you face it all without the preparatory quietness of that wondrous cup of caffeine?

The Psalmist said that "early in the morning he would seek God". There is something powerful about the early morning - those moments before the rest of the world has joined the cacophony of human activity. Jesus Himself rose often early in the morning to be alone with His Father. He knew that if He did not grab those quiet moments to prepare His soul for the day ahead, the needs and demands of people would make it impossible later on. He was determined to get His soul fully caffeinated by communion with His Father above. He never rushed out late, anywhere. He never sped past His disciples to connect with someone higher up the social ladder. He was paced, methodical, and thoughtful about all that He did. But it all hinged on the mornings. Time alone - time to think - time to find rest for His soul.

Purpose each day of your married life to begin that day's adventure with rest in your own souls. Share a cup of coffee... or even tea...but only if the distribution system has broken down and there is not a favored coffee kiosk to be found within a 30 mile radius. :)

Pause to enjoy the communion of a shared life, a shared belief, and a shared family. Speak with faith over the day's demands, and agree to walk together in victory standing on the promises of God. Pray. Fill the house with music and the sounds of worship. Propagate peace.

What was I doing those first 25 years? Running too fast, dashing into my day, and justifying it all by claiming that my "morning person" status left me no time for those who took an extra 10 minutes to rub the sleep from their eyes. Happily, my willful addiction to the beautiful beverage has slowed me down and granted me time to hear more clearly the voice of my Savior who calls me to "lie down in green pastures" and to rest "beside still waters". Our individual devotion is becoming more of a shared devotion. We know the day is too big for us, and without Him, we will sink as we walk on the waters to come. Coffee is just our means toward an end, but a pleasant means at that.

Some bemoan the coffee obsession that has seized our 21st century culture. But I for one am glad to have been swept up in the tide. It is one of the more noble trends.

Rise up early - drink coffee - slow down before you speed up - and be at peace!

Psalm 63:1:2
O God, You are my God;
Early will I seek You;
My soul thirsts for You;
My flesh longs for You
In a dry and thirsty land
Where there is no water.
So I have looked for You in the sanctuary,
To see Your power and glory.

WEEK #7
WHATEVER

There is a classic line in the traditional English wedding vows where a bride and groom pledge their faithfulness in any and all future circumstances. One familiar line declares "for richer or poorer; in sickness and in health"... with the idea being that <u>whatever</u> life throws our way, we will stick by one another. Undoubtedly, an honorable pledge, and one exchanged in my own wedding years ago.

Except believers in Jesus Christ are not stumbling through life enduring "whatever".

We are not uncertain as to our future. All are tried and will face pressure in some way during the course of life - these are earthly realities by which we learn to develop our faith and grow in the grace of God, patience, and maturity. But an even higher reality is that Jesus has paid a very high price to insulate us from the "whatever". Not only is there an escape clause from the "whatever", but there are a series of promises that assure us we have a different destiny than the average person.

Our economic security and our health are not a lottery. Our well-being does not rest in the hands of legislators or kings, but in the resurrection of the only King who really has power. He has established a charter, a bill of rights, that lays out our privileges and pathways. We are not riding upon the roller coaster of "whatever", but we are cushioned during our journey by "all the promises of God, which are 'Yes' and 'Amen' in Jesus Christ". (I Corinthians 1:20)

The potential for poverty is not in our plan or vocabulary. A solid home does not make decisions based on fear. Many young people today refuse to have children, judging it an unaffordable enterprise or an uncertain proposition in an economically unstable world. Others become miserly, petrified for the potential loss of investment or a stock market tumble. They cannot give generously or celebrate life. Everything becomes tied up in knots over the possibility that the bottom will one day drop out.

But remember the words of King David who declared in Psalm 37:25: *"I have lived a full span of life, from youth to old age, but I have never seen those who walk with God abandoned, and I have never seen their children having to beg bread in the streets".*

David, even prior to the promises secured by Jesus, understood that God's people did not live a "whatever" lifestyle. He understood that God was bigger and better than that. God was sure and certain, a loving Father who watched over the wellbeing of His kids. Security and provision were two absolute birthrights for those who lived for God!

Some years ago, we rewrote those wedding vows to read: *"in times of abundance and in times of tested faith"*. Poverty is no longer in our long range forecast. Faith is undoubtedly tested, but the moments of our back being against a wall are only just that - - moments in time, pauses prior to promised provision, opportunities for waters to part before us and for dry pathways of escape to appear. We may not always be swimming in a sea of excess cash, but neither are we sinking in the swamps of lack and hunger.

Never stop believing for God's best in your lives. Expect His abundant provision for the days to come. Ask, and it shall be given unto you. Seek and you will find. Knock, and He is eagerly waiting to open the door to your faith. Dream things that others would not dare to dream. But never forget along the way that it all hinges on priorities. "Seek first the kingdom of God, and His righteousness, and all these things shall be added unto you".

It was the righteous, observed David, whose children were never in lack. How thankful we are to God that through the blood of Jesus' sacrifice we become "the righteous". We could never earn these awesome privileges on our own, but by His success, we are destined as co-inheritors with Him for a lifetime of success and security.

Psalm 34:8-10 "Oh, taste and see that the Lord is good; Blessed is the man who trusts in Him! Oh, fear the Lord, you His saints! There is no want to those who fear Him. The young lions lack and suffer hunger; But those who seek the Lord shall not lack any good thing."

WEEK #8
THE WONDERS OF AN IMPERFECTLY ORDERED LIFE

A man once said to me that he had no time for pets or animals. He said:

"They are an inconvenience and a nuisance, and besides, I can't possibly accomplish what's important if I have to be bothered with keeping track of pets".

I've pondered these words many times, wondering if they indeed had merit. They represent a particularly North American way of thinking which assumes that if something is not perfectly ordered, then it cannot possibly be good. After all, God is a God of order and design. Jesus did nothing by chance, so ought we not also have a handle on every waking moment, maximizing productivity, warring against all things unscheduled, and denouncing every intrusion that knocks us off schedule from our perfectly planned day?

Perfectionism: our calling and our curse. For the Scripture says to "Be perfect as your Heavenly Father is perfect", and again, "He perfects that which concerns us". He is most certainly a God who places high value on perfection. But perfectionism, from another point of view, can work quite the opposite effect upon us.

We find our worth so often in our neatly structured universe, forgetting that as orderly as each one of us might individually be, we inhabit a chaotic planet that does not always cooperate with our schedules and eccentricities. Planes are delayed, vehicles break down, documents vanish, dinners burn, appliances malfunction, luggage goes to Houston while we are heading to Seattle...you get the picture.

And what will happen to your perfectionism when such "imperfection" invades the harmony of your domain? Will you snap at one another, blame, or become agitated and miserable to live with? Or will you learn to laugh and adapt to the ever shifting sands of circumstance? Somewhere there is a firm ground upon which you may rest, but rest assured, it is not to be found in the unfolding of a perfect plan, but rather in the Perfect One who tells us that "in his heart, a man makes his plans; but the Lord's purpose prevails".

Thus enters a cat one day into my perfectly ordered world, shivering one night in the snow, and all my vain pleading to keep the door shut was ignored. For I knew, I simply KNEW that if that door was opened, my future would be forever compromised with litter boxes, veterinarians, hair, sneezing...why on earth would someone want to accommodate all of the above? Also, she did not come alone, for disruptions never do, and as is the nature of glitches in the matrix, her womb carried more drama. And now came kittens; loud and whining Siamese monsters, ready to destroy, at will, all that dangled before their path.

Certainly I am now reformed and chastened back to my former safety net of controllable people being the only welcomed guests into that castle called family? Think again. Not even three months goes by, and the answer to my prayers for an inspiring family gift turns out to be an eight week old Black Labrador Puppy! Think cat chaos times ten! The cat now seems like a non-event next to the schedule shattering realities of a young puppy. Teeth shredded office documents, accidents on the carpet, barking that splits the eardrums; surely I am by now, with this added insult to injury, fully transformed back into resolute resistance toward all things that fail to comply.

But, herein lies the wonders of an imperfect world. For miracle of miracles, I have fallen in love with those whirlwinds of unpredictability, and discovered indeed that all the family, present company included, are much happier with the extra load and administration. For along with them comes the joy of spontaneity that so easily can be lost when we pass from childhood to maturity.

Spontaneity and unplanned craziness: the perfect solution to the chains of perfectionism. Pets are a gift, but others can fill the bill. A relative who drops by unannounced. A lengthy phone call from a needy friend. A stranger in need by the roadside as you, the Good Samaritan, happen to come by. These are the events that add color to a world that we, increasingly as we grow older, attempt to paint completely white. We don't want variety, change, or disruption. But these are often the fountain for our most precious memories.

And so driving one day 31 years ago down a country road in Spain, the unthinkable happened to me, and I became lost; heading ever deeper into the countryside until the road became a lane and the lane became a cow path and the cow path ultimately ended in a field of grass, where cattle mooed in mockery at the panicked perfectionist.

I had planned it all so well, and now it seemed beyond my capacity. I was out of gas, out of faith, and out of answers. But in the chaos came an opportunity for wonder, as my bride began to sing of the faithfulness of God. Backing out of that pasture, I somehow twisted and turned my way back to civilization, driving three more hours on a completely empty tank of gas, until we reached our destination. If my perfection had prevailed, the miracle would have been missed. There would have been no need for God if chaos had not enveloped me that night. Through the darkness came light. Then came laughter, and then came wonder.

Keep your home filled with wonder. Let the unplanned become opportunity for grace to be discovered. Leave some loose ends occasionally untied. Save room for the unexpected. Stay childlike, spontaneous, adventurous, and on the edge. Flee the sterility of perfectionism, and embrace the One who was perfect for you, so that you, as vessels of clay and humility, can freely run your race with a grin on your face and a twinkle in your eye. And remember, no matter how hot an unscheduled desert may seem, a wondrous adventure awaits the faithful on the other side!

Deuteronomy 6:20-22 "When your son asks you in time to come, saying, 'What is the meaning of the testimonies, the statutes, and the judgments which the Lord our God has commanded you?' "Then you shall say to your son: 'We were slaves of Pharaoh in Egypt, and the Lord brought us out of Egypt with a mighty hand; and the Lord showed signs and wonders before our eyes."

WEEK #9
YOURS MINE OR OURS

According to the Scriptures, you've now left parents behind and the "two have become one flesh". That is frankly the easiest bonding that the newlyweds will ever be tasked with. The real challenge begins once the honeymoon is over and the daily routine begins. Then the mysteries of "oneness" begin to unfold.

Most of the time it is fun and adventurous. A friend to eat meals with, plan out the day with, and go to sleep with and wake up to. There are some wonderful advantages to being "one". But the oneness of money is usually not the easiest of adjustments. There are all sorts of theories on how to manage the challenge of shared wealth (or the lack of). Some advocate separate bank accounts, while others take turns managing the bills and spending. With some couples it works best for one partner to be the administrator. What will work best for you?

It is one of the foremost questions for premarital consideration: How will we handle decisions about our money? Don't stumble into this one, because it being the case that the majority of all marital breakdowns are spurred on by financial pressures and conflicts, you don't want to leave this matter to chance or good luck. Human nature doesn't make room for good luck. Being intentionally Biblical will go a long way toward protecting your union from the pitfalls that have tripped up others.

And what does it mean to be Biblical when it comes to our marital money? Simply by extending the principle of the two becoming one, you can establish a firm foundation that will weather any pressure or storm. It is a determination to eradicate self-ownership and control, and an embracing of a higher spiritual principle that in humility we find power, and in abdication we find enthronement.

When I say "I do", I'm also saying "I don't" and "I won't". "I do" means "I no longer live solo, but I now live as a part of you and you now live as a part of me". It means that I don't and I won't claim ownership or independence as my personal right or privilege. My privilege is now to live as your partner, friend, and co-executor of all things over which God gives us dominion. We are a team and we are partners. The money is not yours or mine. Every resource and asset becomes ours, and in becoming ours it likewise becomes God's.

We each might have our individual employment, bank accounts, earnings, or retirement investments, but we don't hoard them or defend them as untouchable by the other. We shun the words "that's mine to do with as I please". We stand or fall together. We dream, sacrifice, invest, lavish, save, and spend together. Our little hobbies and miscellaneous pleasures and purchases don't need microscopic analysis. Liberty is there to act as an individual and to retain our unique and separate interests. But for things that matter, that are sizable, that are serious - in all these areas, we are one.

It matters not whose sweat procured it, whose faith released it, or whose ingenuity extracted it. It all came from God, by grace, and together we are a team of stewards, charged with the principles of peace and partnership which will save us from ever competing over a limited resource.   For in union, and in faith, we recognize the unlimited resources of God, entrusted more and more to those who will care for it according to God's method and plan.

Living as one, not under the gun,
Of conflict and scraping when
bill paying's done;
Don't lose all the fun, by covenant undone,
Financial control is a fantasy spun;

The fretful and anxious forever in fear,
Are certain their personal Doomsday is near,
And so cannot trust any partner with cash,
Demanding, they are, that you hand them the stash;

So vanquish such devils before hearts they soil,
Abundance enjoy and protect it from spoil,
For union, tells Scripture, will bring you fresh oil,
To strengthen your souls and keep tempers from boil;
How blessedly sweet are the ones who agree,
That what's mine is for you, and what's yours is for me.
                                                    R. K. Brake

Psalm 133:
Behold, how good and how pleasant it is for brethren to dwell together in unity!
It is like the precious oil upon the head,
Running down on the beard, the beard of Aaron;
Running down on the edge of his garments.
It is like the dew of Hermon, descending upon the mountains of Zion; For there the Lord commanded the blessing-life forevermore!

WEEK #10
BREAKING BREAD IN BANGLADESH

Yes, a devotional thought from Bangladesh. Like so many other countries these days, Bangladesh is desperate for bread. People work for a wage that puts food on the table, hopefully enough for that one day. People fight for jobs so they can afford bread.

There are all kinds of breads available here - Naan bread, onion bread, flat bread, western style loaves of bread, and on and on. Governments rise and fall on their ability to ensure the people have bread; and at times rice. But starch is the bottom line of nutritional survival: maybe there is little meat, maybe a lack of steady produce, definitely no extra for sweets and soda, but there always has to be bread.

The government of Egypt collapsed some years ago primarily because they could not guarantee a steady stream of subsidized bread. Bakeries ran empty, and 80 million people overthrew a dictatorship of three decades all because it woefully miscalculated the error of depriving people their daily bread.

So here we sit, reading from our Daily Bread: Luke the 7th chapter, for what is probably the 200th time. Acts 7, the story of

Steven's stoning, also read perhaps 100-150 times over. Psalm 7 as well - maybe the 300th or 400th time of reading over this Psalm. Who in the world needs that much bread?

Neglect your soul's need for bread, and the government of our homes can quickly come crashing down. For in our bread we find communion with one another. We find the strength and resource we need to press onward. We find the power to press through another day. We find nurture for the mind, so that our thoughts can process clearly, and not merely react to circumstances in a chaotic clawing for survival. Bread tells the stomach, and then the mind, that everything will be okay for one more day. You cannot make it without bread.

Jesus taught us to pray "Give us this day our daily bread". He rebuked the tempter with the words, "Man shall not live by bread alone (natural bread), but by every word that proceeds from the mouth of God" (spiritual bread). A strong marriage lives by the very words of God. It does not coast from Sunday to Sunday. It does not depend on others to fortify its soul. It feeds itself. It finds daily bread.

The Bible, the Word of God, becomes life, direction, nutrition, and instruction. The Bible gives us wisdom and power to maximize manhood and womanhood, and it demonstrates excellence to transcend the norm and live higher and better than others can even imagine.

Don't go a single day of married life without bread. Chew it over again, for the umpteenth time: that instruction from Ephesians 5 on a revelatory marriage; that lesson in John of Jesus, the Bread of Life; that miracle in all the Gospels of loaves multiplied; the bread that put fire in Elijah's belly in I Kings; that manna in Exodus that sustained a generation; that unleavened Passover bread that heralded a nation's deliverance.

Wherever you find yourselves in days to come, make sure to break bread. Mull over its unique flavor that day. Share your discoveries. Don't keep the aroma a secret. Bread is your security. With its steady supply, your house will stand. No uprising will ever bring you down. Bread will fill you, but then remind you to keep hungering for more. Fresh bread's aroma will mark you. Once you've known it, you cannot live without it.

Even in Bangladesh... or Alaska... or Rome... wherever you may find yourselves in days to come - - eat your fill, eat it again and again, and build yourselves a home that will last all the days of your life.

Matthew 7:24-25 "Therefore, whoever hears these sayings of Mine, and does them, I will liken him to a wise man who built his house on the rock; And the rain descended, the floods came, And the winds blew and beat on that house; And it did not fall, for it was founded on the rock."

WEEK #11
<u>WILL YOU BE MY VALENTINE?</u>

Written February 14, 2014
Some traditions are better left buried in the past. Like the one which compelled school age children to bring sickeningly sweet heart shaped pieces of sugar to class for distribution to their classmates. Or the mandate to supply a corny card for every kid seated with you in the 5th grade, no matter how utterly impossible it was that you would ever end up romantically connected to any of them. Society demanded that its children pretend to be awash with loving kindness every February 14th, and that all humans should have the inalienable right of cards and candy on that most sacred of days.

With tradition ingrained deep into the memory center of our brains, most have not matured beyond this pre-pubescent ritual. Believing that love is best demonstrated by a hastily scrawled card or purchased box of chocolates, they continue to diminish the power of romance by letting card companies dictate their sentiment and the calendar dictate reminders of the importance of keeping the flame alive.

Here are the assumptions of Valentine's Day:

1. It is assumed that all normal people like chocolate. This, actually, is correct. Only psychologically damaged people reject chocolate. But they don't tell you whether true love is found in dark chocolate or milk chocolate. Many a romance has crashed upon the perilous rocks of chocolate preference misinformation. Don't get this wrong, whatever else you do.

2. It is assumed that all can read. To be in love, you must be a devotee of reading. What is the point of a card if you cannot read. You must be skilled in the distinction between sonnet, haiku, and rhyming verse. You must have an advanced degree in English literature. If not, your love can never be articulated properly.

3. The final assumption is that you are chronologically impaired. You do not regard the passage of time, and thus have no clue that it has been 18 years and 7 months since you last said "I love you". Valentine's Day is designed to save the relationships of the linearly disabled.

Shall we revolt and abandon this holiday altogether? No, for in fact the majority need help to rekindle their spark. By nature, our candle dims. We must find fuel for the flame, and learn to apply it liberally. But let us then take society's prompting to another level and discover that the prompting of the Holy Spirit brings much greater creativity, far greater emotional intensity, and a wonderful repetition of acts of kindness that exceed the mid-winter mandate many times over.

He will push us toward reminders of love year round. He is relentless, not only at reminding us repeatedly of the Father's Love, but also at reminding us to distribute what has been received. To walk with God is to live with notifications always turned on. His voice is there to spare us from the plight of the oaf, who fails year after year to acknowledge an anniversary, birthday, or special occasions of other great meaning.

He knows what kind of flowers, cards, or chocolates will speak loudest. He knows that sometimes a shared experience which costs nothing will far exceed in value a purchased prize that cost everything. He knows the power of a look, a twinkle of the eye, a clasping of hands in the setting sun. He knows everything about the one whom you must continue to woo, long after the vows have been exchanged.

He knows the language of love for every human heart. He is called the Teacher, assigned and eager to lead you into all truth - even those truths that seemed locked away tightly into the secret places of the soul. He loves the love of your life more than you ever will! And He is eager to provide you the keys into the most tender places of their heart.

Song of Solomon 2:10-12:
My beloved spoke, and said to me:
"Rise up, my love, my fair one,
And come away.
For lo, the winter is past,
The rain is over and gone.
The flowers appear on the earth;
The time of singing has come,
And the voice of the turtledove
Is heard in our land."

WEEK #12
KATHMANDU'S ROYAL KUMARI,
THE LIVING GODDESS

Peeking out the airplane window at the summit of Everest while flying out of Nepal, my mind is filled with thoughts of Kathmandu's Kumari. I had seen flashes of her on television as she was carried through the streets of the city in her throne-like carriage. Later I learned that her feet never touch the ground outside of her palace, for the duration of her supposed incarnation. Yes, incarnation, as it is tragically believed.

The majority of residents of the capital city hail her as the living embodiment of the Hindu goddess Teleju. She is chosen as a young child following a rigorous selection process. She must be unblemished, have jet black hair and eyes, long eyelashes like a cow, and the "soft voice of a duck"! She is about 5 or 6 years of age at selection, and passes the most severe of tests and examinations, including the necessity of spending a night alone in a room filled with the severed heads of 100 sacrificed goats and cows without showing any trace of fear. Yikes! Pity the poor girl, who, once approved, is then presented to the spirit for inhabitation.

And thus her reign begins, continuing until the time where she passes into puberty. For those 10 years or so, her word is absolute. Other carefully selected children are allowed to play with her in her palace, but only after understanding fully that whatever the Kumari commands is their sacred duty and obligation to do. She may seize their toys, demand her own rules in games, and in general have whatever she wants. Adults come to her for blessings, and her every expression is interpreted for good or evil. If she laughs or cries, you are likely doomed in the near future.

If she shivers, get ready for a trip to prison! If she is perfectly still, only then is your petition assured of success.

How tragic is the fate of this sad child? Poisoned from the earliest age with thoughts of her own divinity; spoiled hopelessly with the scepter of absolute authority, believing that it is her divine right to have her want and way in every situation of life; sending adults into a trembling panic if her disapproval is aroused.

Hmmm.....I've seen such a child a few places before: in the aisles of grocery stores screaming for the treats to which they believe they are entitled, holding their parents hostage in restaurants by running amok and daring them to risk public discipline, or incapable when playing with other kids of handling loss, disadvantage, or domination. These have been, like the Kumari, deceived into believing they are the center of the universe and the rightful focus of every adult's admiration.

And herein lies the challenge for the married couple, for such children, unrestrained or untrained, will inevitably seek to conquer and divide their parents. The brat unbridled leads to blame and embarrassment. Who is responsible for the emotional mayhem of this maniacal miniaturization of domestic authority? Which of us failed to steer and direct their path? Who pampered them in private, or placated them with privilege, while the other alone wielded the rod and thus became unwillingly the object of their infantile resentment?

No, dear parents to be, you dare not bring another Kumari upon an innocent and unsuspecting world. A few points of advance agreement will work wondrously toward reigning in your blessing's baser instincts. Wisdom and knowledge, provided by the Scriptures, will save a world of frustration and conflict both in the home and out in society. Here are a few tips for vanquishing any Kumari who would attempt to turn your peaceful home into his or her own personal palace:

1. Be honest with yourself, and agree with God that your kids have not been born perfect. They have, in fact, inherited Adam's nature, as have mom and dad. They will inevitably push the boundaries as far as possible, if not restrained, trained, and programmed in their brain!

2. Children can be lavished with love and blessings, yet still learn early the meaning of the word "NO". Many adults cannot manage both sides of the formula. They either are too heavy-handed, fearing to be overly gracious, or they are too pampering, fearing to damage their child through denial. God's wisdom balances both.

3. Let your darling learn early on they will never come between mom and dad. The two of you together form an impenetrable wall of agreement. Once they've faced this wall repeatedly and discovered that it has no cracks, they will ultimately tire of attempting to breach it.

4. Teach them early the joy and empowerment of honoring and exalting others. Let them see humility working in the home as their parents refuse entitlement, and use their earthly position and resource for the uplifting of people. The sooner their little

feet touch ground in a place of commonality and service among their own peers, the more whole they will become as adults.

5. Never find your own fulfillment through the visibility of your child. Many a mom or dad has sat basking in the limelight as their little one proceeded to hijack the public atmosphere of a church service or restaurant. Find your identity in God, but not through the attention your child can command through unbridled commotion.

Little darlings indeed, but not goddesses or gods. Glorious gifts from God, but not granted immunity to parade with impunity. They are the greatest natural joys you can have in this life, but be sure that others are not secretly denouncing your treasure as their torment.   And in so doing, your children will be jewels in your crown and in the eyes of all around you.

"Then the mother of Zebedee's sons came to Him with her sons, kneeling down and asking something from Him. And He said to her, "What do you wish?" She said to Him, "Grant that these two sons of mine may sit, one on Your right hand and the other on the left, in Your kingdom."......; But Jesus called them to Himself and said, "You know that the rulers of the Gentiles lord it over them, and those who are great exercise authority over them. Yet it shall not be so among you; but whoever desires to be great among you, let him be your servant......; Just as the Son of Man did not come to be served, but to serve......"   Matthew 20:20, 25, 27

WEEK #13
DON'T LET THE SUN GO DOWN

Here is a Scripture that is often tough to obey: *"Don't let the sun go down on your wrath". (Ephesians 4:26)* Wrath is in itself a pretty tough word. Have you ever felt full of wrath with your beloved? Probably not, but anger, irritation, and frustration are common to all. The same text is preceded with the words "in your anger, do not sin". We are being cautioned then about an anger that has been taken too far.

You cannot live with another human being and not have moments or perhaps even extended episodes of unpleasant feeling and exchange. Some enter into the marriage covenant and become quickly shocked or dismayed by how rapidly the romance can dissipate into an all-out war of words. Disappointed, they either retreat into a quiet corner to ponder the imminent end of the world, or they take the bait and ratchet things up a few notches, fueling their indignation with volume or tears.

What wisdom is God attempting to impart to us with this command to make a quick end to our feuding? Is it simply a law to keep us in line, or perhaps rather a token of grace? Or is it some gentle counsel from our Father who desires us to "as much as possible, live at peace with all men".

Peace is one of the three core components of the kingdom of God (Romans 14:17). Peace is in the fruit basket of the Holy Spirit. Peace is the promise extended by Jesus before His departure. (John 14:27) A peaceful mind, a peaceful home, and peaceful relationships are at the very core of our covenant privileges.

When we are instructed to resolve matters before sunset, it is not so much a demand, but rather a nudge back toward the glorious life of privilege that all who call upon Jesus are given to enjoy. We do not have to war. Fighting like cats and dogs is not inevitable. Screaming matches are not part and parcel of a "healthy home". Demoralizing disputation is not predestined. Two very different people, both as followers of Christ, can have shown unto them "a better way".

There is a wonderful verse that says "He gives His beloved rest". (Psalm 127:2) A sound night's sleep is one of the blessings of faith. It is restorative and recuperative. It keeps the body from burn out and the soul from weariness. This is one reason the enemy of your soul loves for you to take bitterness to bed. He loves for you to lie awake in fear and anxiety. Filling the mind with doubt over the long term health of your relationship is another of his favorite strategies. Take the conflict to bed, and you will be guaranteed to awake with it ringing more loudly than your morning alarm.

Consider a few practicalities of early resolution, rather than burying things until the next day:

Hashing things out while exhausted is a recipe for trouble. The end of the day is the time of minimal energy for the majority. They have already expended themselves, and their best has been given. You need the best of your mental and spiritual energy for conflict resolution.

Light is comforting. Darkness can feel so condemning. Sunshine brings hope, but darkness can lead to despair. Don't lie in bed in the dark with thoughts running wild. Things always seem so much bigger and scarier in the dark.

Scripture teaches us that aspects of God's nature are seen through the created world. Since we need to be "Godly" with our words and thoughts when resolving disputes, try getting outside and walking it through in the light of day. A few moments at the beach or a park, or with a majestic mountain vista before us, can calm our soul and bring perspective.

Holding your problem up to the light of God's majesty can restore perspective and keep issues from spiraling out of control. It is good to step back and take a good look at God, rather than being obsessed with the momentary size of our relational misstep.

Forgiveness is always urgent! Never postpone forgiveness. An offense (carried over) troubles our own soul even more than it troubles the one who has offended us. Free yourself while you can still see and think clearly.

Change the goal. We don't need to see eye to eye on every subject. But we do need to walk heart to heart. Our distinctions don't have to divide us.

Keep chasing daylight. Some things are indeed a grounds for anger or frustration. Jesus became both angry and disturbed by relational disconnection during his three covenant years of work with His disciples. But He never stewed, yelled, ranted, or humiliated. He resolved matters, quickly, by the wisdom of the Counselor who resided within Him, and by the determination to let no God-ordained relationship slip through His hands.

His disciples, though frighteningly flawed, were nevertheless precious gifts from God, to assist Him in His mission. Every day's conclusion brought a review of lessons learned and wisdom gained, a fresh determination to begin the day ahead with a clean slate, and the joy of a fellowship unmarred by hidden resentment. For those who love His ways, He offers the power to enjoy the same

For you were once darkness, but now you are light in the Lord. Walk as children of light. For the fruit of the Spirit is in all goodness, righteousness, and truth, finding out what is acceptable to the Lord. But all things that are exposed are made manifest by the light, for whatever makes manifest is light. Therefore He says: "Awake, you who sleep, arise from the dead, and Christ will give you light." Ephesians 5:8-10, 13-14

WEEK #14
PRAYER: AND WHY IT DOESN'T ALWAYS WORK

This seems like a rather irreverent title for a devotional, does it not? We are taught from our earliest years that God answers prayer and that prayer works. Prayer is the foundation, the key, the wall of protection around our union. But they forgot to tell us that it is also one of the more challenging things a couple will ever do together.

Prayer most certainly works, and God most certainly answers prayer. But it is the work of prayer where most find their point of stumbling.

In counseling Christian couples, we find that most do not have a shared prayer life. This is strange. They are good people, and if interviewed, may both profess their strong belief in God and in the importance of prayer. But for the majority, prayer is intensely private, and uncomfortable when shared in the inner chambers of the home.

Let us understand ourselves, and why it takes discipline to come together in prayer. A man and a woman, married, share a degree of intimacy that is unmatched in any other human bond. There is no one we are more closely bonded with than our spouse. Why, then, does prayer often become a brick wall between two who are so intertwined?

The reason lies in the higher intimacy, the relationship that far surpasses in depth and union even that between husband and wife. It is the relationship between each one of us and our Creator. It is a bond of the spirit realm, not one of body or soul alone. The realm of the Spirit is the most intimate realm. God is Spirit, and we relate to Him and commune with Him spirit to Spirit. It is here that nothing is hidden. There is no artificiality that can mislead Him. It is here that we are most fully known, both where we are weak, and where we are strong. Everything done or thought in the dark is made manifest in the light. God is light, and in Him there is no darkness, no secrets, and no posturing; just total transparency.

And herein lies our problem: we can't fake it in front of God. We are totally exposed in His presence, seen fully for who we are. And though we are washed in the blood of His Son's forgiveness, and He sees us robed in righteousness, we ourselves know the areas of life and thought where we still struggle.

Our spouse, too, knows much of our weakness. Pious prayers will not carry the day in front of family. Family knows the good, the bad, and the ugly. Self-righteousness dies, and the pride of position cannot stand before Him. And so we become vulnerable, weak, and humble...and the one set of things we hate to be in front of our spouse is vulnerable, weak, and humble!

If there is insincerity in our relationship with God, it will manifest in our inability to pray. If we are conflicted in our spiritual identity, it will be exposed in our lack of confidence before His throne. The title of "Christian" suddenly means little. It is where we are at on the inside, with Him, that truly matters.

Shared prayer is shared dependence upon God. It is the realm where no one is right...where the "rightness" of God is all that matters. It is a place where unforgiveness cannot endure. Anger cannot follow us into prayer. Jealousy and resentment have to flee.

All of our pettiness and self-focus suddenly are swallowed up when we approach Jesus who gave His all on Calvary. Everything that hinders and weakens marriage is petrified by the presence of God. Prayer forces us to get right and to be right with one another. It compels us to honor. It invites submission. It unmasks secrecy. It prevents passivity.

Prayer is a marvelous opportunity for us to grow together. If only we can just push past the stage of "awkward" and into the freedom of a shared need for God. If we can overcome our fear, and engage in the work of prayer, we will find that prayer does work, and God will answer. The thing that makes people most uncomfortable in the beginning is the thing that will bring the greatest comfort and peace in the end.

Here are some simple ideas for jump-starting the journey of a marital prayer life:

- Pray briefly - don't put each other to sleep
- Pray naturally - don't use church lingo in your bedroom. No one is falling for it!
- Pray conversationally - talk to God as if you are on a 3-way conference call
- Pray dependently - acknowledge your shared need for God.

- Pray thankfully - the discipline of dinner time "giving thanks" is a great reminder that God is good, and we are totally trusting in Him for all that we have.
- Pray compassionately - for one another's needs, burdens, or infirmities. Minister grace to each other through prayer
- Pray confidently - don't wallow in self-pity or shame; you are children of God, and He answers us because of His Son's righteousness, not our own. We don't have to be perfect to get our prayers answered...just persistent!
- Pray progressively - building a life of shared prayer is a lifetime project. Don't beat yourself up for missed goals or short time frames. Anything you accomplish together in prayer is way more than what most are accomplishing.
- Pray simply - don't try to impress God or your spouse. We are all kids in His presence.

Now this is the confidence that we have in Him, that if we ask anything according to His will, He hears us, and we know that if He hears us, whatever we ask, we know that we have the requests that we have asked of Him. I John 5:14-15

WEEK #15
SMALL BEGINNINGS

Back in the day, a young couple was delighted to start out with a small room, perhaps a bed and a few secondhand furnishings. Articles for the household were slowly assembled over a period of time, rarely by borrowing, but rather most always by careful saving and scrimping, until the cherished TV or living room chair could be purchased with cash. We live today in a very different time. It is an age of instant gratification where no desire is delayed, and where people don't want to wait months, let alone years, to acquire something that their heart is set upon. The urge to accumulate quickly has brought great strain on many relationships, and the freedom of a simplified life has been lost.

There is a great freedom in simplicity. There is something magical about working hard together and taking pride in those early hard earned purchases or adornments for our homes. I well remember the first piece of furniture we purchased, a couch for $300, the wedding gift of a generous relative. It was so much fun going out and shopping for that perfect addition to our tiny living room. Little did we know it would be years before we ever bought another piece of furniture.

Items accumulated through the gifts of others or by gleaning the cast offs of another person's overflow. We never felt poor, and we were content with what we had. But gradually, and naturally, possessions began to increase and we became blessed with things we never imagined ourselves owning. Faithfulness to God brings a measure of prosperity into all of our lives. Those who are good stewards of little are entrusted with much. It is a Biblical principle, and there is no fault in walking in it.

But how very important it is that we not forget the power of our humble beginnings. It was in those times of leanness that we discovered the amazing faithfulness of our God. Things hard won bring a much longer lasting joy. When we have paid a price for something, we appreciate it so much more. If everything falls into our laps, we are not by human nature very skilled at keeping sanity and perspective. We spoil quickly, and our gratitude can quickly turn into a demand for entitlement.

It is wise to build slowly and firmly a foundation that will last well into the future. It is good to have a journey of faith together, trusting God for the things that are outside our grasp. Too quickly the credit cards and banks of today can become the Egyptian saviors of long ago. They have their place, but let them never tempt us to make them our gods. We have only one true source, and it has been well said that "God will do better for you than you will ever do for yourself." Working hard, and trusting in His timing is a marvelous pattern for building a stable material life together.

Do not despise the day of small beginnings. Zechariah 4:10

WEEK #16
YOUR WONDERFUL MOTHER-IN-LAW

Yes indeed, Mothers-in-Law are awesome! Despite rumors to the contrary, it is a blessing to have a second mother added into your life. Both husband and wife will have this joy. Some say the son-in-law has it worse, and others think the greater burden is on the daughter-in-law. In truth, it depends not so much on the mother-in-law, but on you!

There are all sorts of mothers-in-law; some sweet, some respectful, some nosing and some imposing. None of them will be perfect, but whatever they may be, you as the son-in-law or daughter-in-law have a great opportunity to practice the heart of Jesus and bring a touch of joy to one who has spent her whole life preparing your spouse for your embrace, only to have to watch you walk away with him or her in the end. Mothers are the ultimate "sacrificers" and servants. They do the hard work for 18 years physically and then years added on spiritually, and you waltz in and claim the fruit of their labor. Should not such a woman be crowned with gold and rewarded with your allegiance?

A guiding light is the admonition of Scripture to "honor your father and mother that your days may be long upon the earth." It is the only commandment with a specific promise attached. One discovers that it applies first to our natural parents, but then God extends this to those who enter into a parental role in our lives.

By becoming one with your spouse, their parents become yours. Her mom becomes another mom to love, look after, and pamper. His mother is no longer competition, but one whose heart can be made glad as she sees from afar her baby prospering in your loving care. It is a tall order to be an excellent spouse, but it is an even taller order to be an excellent member of a family you did not grow up in.

Perhaps it seems that we are doing enough just by loving one another. But God's grace is without limitation. There is enough in God to empower us for all kinds of added family. We may get new brothers and sisters, nieces and nephews, cousins, aunts and uncles. We cannot and dare not think that "they are not my problem since I only married YOU!" For in fact when we married, we got the whole package... a new family history, family genes, family joys and family sorrows. But let us not get ahead of ourselves; we are speaking today simply of the mother-in-law.

She is a queen whose labor must always be remembered. She crafted the one whom you now call your own. She prayed and contended for you as the future spouse of her beloved daughter or son. She dreamed and envisioned, counseled and prayed, changed your diapers and sat up through nights of sickness and heartache. She loved unconditionally even when you did not love yourself. She trusted your choices and then let you fly. There is no one quite like your mother, and no one quite like your mother-in-law.

Oh, what to do with such a woman! She sometimes cannot help herself, offering unsolicited bits of advice or wisdom, raising an eyebrow over your methods of keeping the home (or not); she has a vested interest in your success, your future children, your continued health and prosperity. She cannot simply "mind her own business", for there is no business that will ever cross her mind that will surpass (in importance) the business of her offspring's future and destiny.

She must be tenderly tolerated if she wanders too closely in; she must be remembered on every occasion as the one who paid the highest price of any family member. She, too, craves special gifts and thoughts, and every chance to be welcomed at a meal or a family event is a treasure that she counts down toward. Even when forgotten, she will never forget the birthdays, the anniversaries, the favorite foods, colors and fragrances. It is her business to remember, and remember she will do with excellence.

And so let us remember our beloved mother-in-law. Let us ponder the pathways to flooding her heart with joy. And when we bless mama, we simultaneously bless our spouse, for who does not rejoice to see their beloved mother refreshed and crowned with the glory she so richly deserves.

My mother-in-law loved two simple things in life: cashews and mint milk chocolate. I bore them proudly with every visit. She drove me crazy in lots of ways with her eccentricities and gentle nagging, but she gave me her daughter, my beloved wife. I devoted myself to thanking her for that all the days of her life. In the end, she adored me and knew I loved her. I could make her laugh. And for that I have a lot of peace before God. It is good to send someone home to their heavenly reward and to know that you held nothing back from them. It is also good for your own longevity. Honor God first. Honor your spouse second. And make sure that your beloved mothers are not too far behind!

"And Orpah kissed her mother-in-law, but Ruth clung to her. And she said, 'Look, your sister-in-law has gone back to her people.....return after your sister-in-law'. But Ruth said: "Don't ask me to leave you, or to turn back from following after you; for wherever you go, I will go, and wherever you lodge, I will lodge; your people shall be my people, and your God my God."
Ruth 1:14-16

WEEK #17
ON THE VIRTUES OF MINIATURE GOLF

Now here is a true American phenomenon, the addiction of millions of families to the mindless sport of miniature golf. There have been numerous historical moments associated with this pastime. It is said that Abraham Lincoln's assassin was in a state of despondency after losing to his twin brother in an 18 hole playoff round, but I'm not entirely sure that this fits the historical chronology of golf's evolution from Scotland to the Americas.

I myself have flirted with despair when being trumped in the year 2012 by my aging mother's three holes in one. And none will forget my one and only broken bone, a cracked cuboid in my left ankle incurred when crashing to the bottom of the 18th green on the pirate adventure course in Myrtle Beach. A crash that took place because I was tied in score with one of my youth group teens and needed a hole in one to win the trophy. I raced along following my ball down the hill, tripped on a three inch high brick wall, my head smashing to the ground at eye level with the cup, only to watch triumphantly as the ball rolled in. Shredded elbows, broken cuboid, and flattened head...but oh the joy of triumphing over my charges in the wondrous game of miniature golf!

An analysis of this hard core sport can reveal its beloved status among vacationing families, and teach us a few life lessons along the way. Why is it so popular, and why should we preserve its hallowed traditions? For one, it is the great equalizer. Not all our family members are born with the exact same genetic advantages or traits: some are fast and coordinated; some are thinkers and not much into sweat. Some can swing a bat and others can play an instrument. Whatever our strengths, or weaknesses, it seems that just about anyone can turn in a decent round of miniature golf, even if by accident.

The most skilled can blow it, and the most awkward can sink one lucky shot after another. Pride fails utterly on the fairways, where the putter is foiled by the lips and turns and bumps that are meant to amuse, but end up sending the most confident into crazed rants of injustice. Meanwhile, the one who never wins at anything has a marvelous shot at walking away with the victor's crown. Families, in the world of miniature golf, find a marvelous unity in shared incompetence and blind luck. Laughter and lighthearted mockery are routine. No one ever feels a fool for doing poorly in miniature golf, but a random hole-in-one can promote the underdog to hero for the day.

Mini golf is the great killer of ruthless competition. It reminds us that time together is what counts, not domination and scorecards. Little kids have just as great a time as moms and dads. Young couples are often seen on these outings, finding some shared romance in the calmness of a pleasant day, where no one is in a hurry, everyone is tolerant of little children picking up the ball with their hands, strange creatures lurk in the surrounding pools of water, and we don't really care that the putter is never the right size. The point is shared innocence, pure amusement without moral violation, and the joyous reminder that life was not supposed to have become so stress filled and complex.

Miniature golf must never be outgrown. The quest to remain childlike is a worthy one. Life has a way of hardening the arteries and conspiring to deprive us of simplicity and rest. But for the Christian, life is a quest to enter into a wonderful rest in God. We look for medium that will bring equilibrium into our relationships and home.

There is something about mini-golf that reflects the kingdom of grace, where failure is not fatal, and where humbling brings rejoicing, not resentment. We applaud the success of others, and do not mind when a "little child shall lead them." We laugh at ourselves, while striving ever more fervently to perfect our craft. What a brilliant picture of kingdom living! Who does not want to attain unto perfection, and is not the "hole-in-one" the zenith of emotional euphoria and moral exaltation? Yet rare is the hole-in-one, but somehow joy is still there.

We miss the mark, but head home after a round or two feeling like kings of the hill. We spent time breathing fresh air, loving our family members and friends, laughing at our own humanity, and cheering one another on with each valiant effort. At little cost we received great gain. But even with the price spiraling upward annually, we return again and again. It is the ultimate bargain, a lifetime of relational memories for the price of a fast food meal.

Husband and wife, I challenge you to return regularly to those humbling hills of holistic hilarity. Find those activities in life that quench continually the false fires of relational ambition and marital competition. Keep your life simple, keep your recreation pure. Cheer one another on, and forever keep believing that the next hole will surely be your soulmate's hole-in-one. Strive to win the prize, but remember: in this game, the one who scores lowest is the real winner in the end!

"There remains therefore a rest for the people of God. For he who has entered His rest has himself also ceased from his own labors as God did from His. Let us therefore be diligent to enter that rest..." Hebrews 4:8-11a

WEEK #18
BEST FRIENDS

While growing up as a kid, I was often asked the question at school "Who is your best friend? It seemed to be the social preoccupation of elementary and junior high school children. Everyone wanted to know who you most preferred, who you spent your "most fun" moments with, or who you laughed with the most. The question I'm sure was prompted by shallower motivations such as competition or jealousy. But it remains to this day an important question, for reasons of greater substance.

Today, it is a more complex question. I am asked at times by my children or colleagues "Who is your closest confidant or most intimate friend?" They are each referring to my collection of male friends, those I spend the most time with on the phone or visit most frequently. Among men, there is no longer an all-around "best" as different friends are valued for different areas of strength that they bring to my life. Some are the greatest asset to my spiritual growth, while others bring out the greatest refreshing through laughter. Some are favorite partners for travel or ministry, while others are trusted confidants. I really don't have a "best" male friend anymore, but rather a collection of closest friends. A group of men, whom taken together, are the very best of my friends.

But having a best, or closest, or most trusted friend is in fact one of the essentials of a healthy life. Most people don't know that Jesus had a best friend. He was the disciple John, the "one whom Jesus loved." Jesus entrusted to John the care of his mother, the most cherished relationship in his earthly life. Jesus allowed John a greater level of intimacy and shared with him more deeply. Jesus had many disciples, a core group of followers, three in his inner circle (Peter, James, and John), but only one of those three was his closest confidant. You can only have one best friend.

King David had a best friend. His name was Jonathan, the son of Saul. David and Jonathan loved one another and watched one another's back. When David did not know whom to trust, he knew he could trust Jonathan. Their relationship survived many challenges and storms. Best friends are like that. They stick by you no matter what. When everything else turns against you, your best friend remains by your side.

I am so thankful today that I learned early on that my spouse was intended by God to become my best friend, and indeed, for 32 years of marriage she has been exactly that. I know in fact the immediate answer to "who is your best friend?" I don't have to think about it or compare the various virtues of my closest colleagues. My wife is, not by necessity, but in reality, my very best friend.

And this I believe is an option available to all who make Christ central to their marriage. The two become one flesh, but they become so much more than one flesh. They have an opportunity to be joined in heart, in soul, in mind, and in body. They receive the privilege of discovering friendship at a deeper level than most will ever know in this life. Their shared bond in the Holy Spirit allows them to commune on a plane unfamiliar to those who unite around the more temporal things such as shared hobbies or sports. It is so rewarding and safe to have a spouse as a best friend, and it is worth the lifetime of labor that is required to build such a precious and life enhancing relationship.

So how does it happen, and why do most who are married fail to attain this joy? Is it simply a matter of "being a good match," or can we cultivate this garden and make it more fertile and rewarding? Must my spouse be my best friend by obligation, or is it possible, with any couple, for this to be developed intentionally and naturally?

Here are a few simple principles for enhancing friendship in the home and for building for yourselves the security that comes when the marriage relationship is the most rewarding relationship...the relationship that brings the most safety, laughter, and joy:

1. Jesus called his disciples "friends" because "everything He heard from His father he shared with them." In other words, friendship deepens through disclosure. Let your spouse be the one who knows more about your heart than anyone else. Run from the temptation to find your confidant outside the home. But, be sure that you are someone safe to share with. Are you an avid listener? Be the hearing and trustworthy friend that your spouse needs you to be.

2. Don't "out" your spouse in public, or even with other close friends in private. Protect your wife's or husband's dignity, and never share with others their weaknesses or struggles. Your spouse must know that you are their greatest protector, and you will never divulge their secrets to a world with itching ears. How many times have we heard Christians in public settings share their frustration or disappointment with their spouse? Too many times. It is such a breach of trust. Your best friend will be the one who knows that you will never risk their reputation. You are their guardian, and their secrets are locked up and protected within your heart.

3. Join together with your beloved in doing those things that are nearest and dearest to their hearts. Do they love to hike or read or watch movies? If so, then do so with them. Don't drift, as so many do, into separate lives, hobbies, and pleasures. Find as many things as possible that you can enjoy doing together.

In short, trust and confidence are the greatest factors in an enduring relationship. Security in knowing that you are loved for who you are (for which reason friendship with God trumps all other relationships, because no one can ever love us as perfectly and unconditionally as God). Total acceptance. Constant availability. A source of joy and laughter. Someone to sit quietly with, without awkwardness. Someone who listens, without growing weary. One who believes the best. John was all of these to Jesus. Jonathan was true to the end for David. You too, can choose to be the best of friends.

"Then the Lord said, 'hear now My words; if there is a prophet among you, I, the Lord, make Myself known to him in a vision; I speak to him in a dream. Not so with my servant Moses; He is faithful in all My house. I speak with him face to face." / "and the Lord talked to Moses face to face, as a man speaks to his friend." Numbers 12:6-8 / Exodus 33:11

WEEK #19
"THIS HOUSE IS CLEAN"

There was a crazy movie back in the 80's called Poltergeist. A key character in the movie was a short little lady who supposedly had the power to detect whether or not a house was free of the influence of evil spirits. When the house had passed her inspection and approval, she would pronounce in a sober and authoritative high pitched voice, "this house is clean." It became a bit of a joke for some years thereafter.

Fast forward to the year 2014. Statistics tell us that 80% of American homes are carrying some form of debt, and the majority are carrying significant debt. There are two primary types of debt, secured and unsecured. A secured debt is considered a reasonable or responsible type of loan, because the lender has the security of your home or vehicle or other asset which protects their interests in case you default.

An unsecured loan would be the type commonly taken from a credit card or bank (or from a nervous looking guy in a seedy "get cash fast" business who dispenses your money from behind bullet proof glass - - don't go to that guy!), where there is no physical asset that you can fall back on if you fail to pay. In this kind of loan, you are borrowing against your future, with the hope, expectation, or prayer, that funds will continue to flow and you won't be left with a bad credit rating due to failure to pay. The majority of our homes in the 21st century are said to be carrying dangerously high levels of unsecured debt.

Okay, all of this loan information might be giving you a headache...exactly! Consider (as shared previously) that financial pressure or debt is the #1 reason given for marital stress or breakup. It is the primary reason some very wonderful couples will submit to explain why they are unable to fulfill their dreams of Christian service or missionary outreach. It is the reason why most feel they cannot tithe to their local church.

Which is precisely the reason why many spiritual counselors who work to help people with their finances have come to the conclusion that there is a "spirit" or "principality" that provokes, tempts, or draws people into unmanageable debt. Just as we recognize there are evil spirits that tempt people in other areas of life, such as lust or greed or bitterness, so we can also surmise that some foul spirit out there has been assigned the task of bringing God's people into the bondage of controlling debt.

It is now being viewed not only as a materialistic urge or craving for comfort, but there are patterns of compulsion and addiction that are recognizable in many of the homes encumbered with loads of unsecured debt. People find themselves unable to stop. They cut up their cards in the same way as the heavy drinker pours out his alcohol in a bid for sobriety, but the fact is soon uncovered that if our heart has not changed, and if we have not been internally and spiritually liberated from the power of what was driving us, we will simply buy another bottle, or apply for another piece of plastic.

There is ample evidence indeed that dark forces are at work across our nation and even in most developing nations now, conspiring to bring young couples and middle-aged families into financial slavery. This steals their joy, deprives them of their peace, and prohibits them from answering God's awesome call to go and to give as His Spirit sends and inspires.

Apparently, the little Poltergeist lady was onto something, but if she was employed to sniff out oppression today, she would rarely find a house deemed "clean." We've been stupefied, seduced, and padlocked into a prison of "must have" that keeps many from the destiny for which they were born. The Scriptures tell us that "the borrower is servant to the lender." He is not completely free.

Jesus wants us liberated in every area: our heart, our emotions, our physical health, and our finances. Our handling of finances is one of the most spiritually telling habits in our life. It is an area where God desires to give us true and overcoming victory. It is an area where many are paralyzed by fear, but where the children of God can flourish, prosper (sufficiency of God's resources for the fulfillment of every purpose that He has for your life), and abound (overflow) unto the accomplishing of numerous good works. It is a wondrous joy to be free to give freely. It is a delight to be able to help others with an interest free loan, a gift, or a blessing that flows freely from our unrestrained hands.

We would not agree, as some contend, that it is a sin or a failure to borrow money. The Scriptures speak often of those who are in a position where they need assistance. The Year of Jubilee is spoken of, where debts are canceled and obligations are lifted. Jesus Himself came proclaiming "the year of the Lord's favor" or "the acceptable year of the Lord," where mankind would become permanently able to live in the overflowing grace and provision of God, for spirit, soul, and body.

The New Testament speaks to us of the posture of those who had become enslaved or indebted by means of necessity for providing for their families as strangers in a foreign land, or when famine or lack of work compelled their dependence. We are not to judge harshly those who have experienced such hard times, and we are admonished to extend grace and mercy as much as possible. Those in debt are not condemned, but those in debt are envisioned for freedom by a God who has the power to set men free.

What shall we conclude regarding debt, in light of these things:

1. Let us not take it lightly. When debt becomes a runaway train, it can run our marriage right off the tracks.

2. We know what we are dealing with. An incidental or convenient use of plastic is not a moral or ethical issue. But a compulsive use for personal gratification may very well indicate that we are listening to whispers that originate from a mind outside our own. Let us "test ourselves, and see whether we are found to be in a place of faith" with our thinking.

3. Let's make sure our house is "clean." Let us be reasonable and wise in our purchases and major borrowing decisions. Let us not gamble with our future, or with the future of our children. "Children should not have to save up for their parents, but parents for their children." II Corinthians 12:14

4. Let us fight the good fight of faith. It is a spiritual battle to have a heart that stays free from covetousness. Let us be content with simplicity in life, for the joys of shared experiences can never be equalled by any material gain

"And God is able to make all grace abound toward you, that you, always having all sufficiency in all things, may have an abundance for every good work. As it is written: 'He has dispersed abroad, he has given to the poor; his righteousness endures forever. Now may He who supplies seed to the sower, and bread for food, supply and multiply the seed you have sown and increase the fruits of your righteousness, while you are enriched in everything resulting in maximum generosity, which causes thanksgiving through us to God." II Corinthians 9:9-11

WEEK #20
KEEP THOSE KIDS COMING

Okay, I'm going to have to start this one with a disclaimer: I have become a grandfather for the first time this week, and therefore I am biased, emotionally intoxicated, and completely non-objective. That being said, I will nevertheless endeavor to be entirely Biblical here on what has become a rather intense issue in the 21st century: "Is it still a good idea to brings kids into this crazy and increasingly unstable world?"

Back in the day, it was almost a non-issue; young couples that got married were expected to start churning out children almost immediately. Those who chose not to were few and far between, and those who could not (for physical reasons) endured an endless stream of insensitive comments from relatives and friends.

Today, however, we find an increasing number of couples who either choose not to have children, or will argue forcefully for the limitation of family size. Whereas in the past, families with large broods were celebrated (more hands to work around the farm), today, there is frequent criticism leveled at those who are "contributing to world overpopulation, being financially irresponsible, or endangering the welfare of young lives by subjecting them to a morally deteriorating climate." Is there a truth somewhere in the middle? How can a young Christian couple process through the pressures of the 21st century and make healthy decisions about the future size of their household? Does God have something to say?

Let us establish a FIRST and foremost principle, which is this: it is the sole right of the couple, humanly speaking, to make these decisions. Whatever their reasoning, whatever their motives, whatever their conclusions, no one should judge or critique the conclusions drawn. Especially since we are not the ones who will have to bring up children in that home, provide for those children, have faith for their spiritual development and health, and basically devote our entire existence to their future and well-being! It is no small decision, and it is profoundly life changing, whether we bring one, two, three or more to share space with seven billion others on this planet.

The second principle is this: Our lives belong to God. His perspective and His vision for our homes and our potential impact on this earth should above all else be our foremost consideration. This only works if we have grasped the thought that "our lives are not our own, and we were bought with a price." Short of that revelation, God's involvement in the determination of household size seems ludicrous to the majority.

But it is the absence of God's involvement that is, in fact, ludicrous. Maybe the naysayers, outside of a God perspective, do have a point. Mankind is fast devouring this planet's resources, cities are overcrowded, and life is becoming more expensive with fewer and fewer opportunities in the natural for the generation that is upcoming. I would not want to embark upon family planning in today's world without being very conscious of my present and future need for God! OK, we all agree that we need God, or we wouldn't be reading or writing marriage devotionals!

Let's get to the point of summarizing some Biblical thoughts on family planning:

- "Children are a heritage from the Lord; the fruit of the womb is a reward." Psalm 127:3   This is rather self-explanatory.   Under any circumstance, kids are not a nuisance, but a gracious gift from God

- "Like arrows in the hands of a warrior, so are the children of one's youth." Psalm 127:4 Kids extend our influence and impact in life. They enable us to continue making a difference long after we are gone.

- Children CAN do well, even in a morally deteriorating world climate. The principles of God's word work in any and every stage of history: "Train up a child in the way he should go, and when he is old, he will not depart from it." Proverbs 22:6

- Children, in their innocence, remind us of the simplicity of faith. They keep us from becoming jaded or cynical. One of the great tragedies of life is when older people choose to move into residential areas that refuse the entry of children. Without the laughter, joy, and purity of children, the world will indeed become an increasingly cold and unfriendly place.

- God's promises to provide for our necessities, and even to grant the desires of our hearts, were never qualified by family size or limited to particular dollar amounts. He is a Provider, period! Let us never allow the absence of faith or fear, regarding finances, to become the determining factor in our choices about family size.

- God actually has a longing for children who are born into spiritually healthy homes. This is a part of His strategy for expanding His kingdom. This is one of the reasons He gives for the tragedy of divorce...it can disrupt healthy spiritual development in the lives of future men and women of faith. "Did He not make them (man and woman) one, having a remnant of the Spirit? And why one? Because He seeks godly offspring. Therefore watch carefully over your own spirit, and do not deal unfaithfully with the wife of your youth." (Malachi 2:15)

There is probably no more important natural decision a young couple will make than the decision of whether or not to have kids, and if so, how many to bring into this world. It is your decision to make. It has much to do with what you believe God has called you to be or to do with your time here on planet earth. Let no one judge you or pressure you with timing, numbers, or human wisdom. Walk with God, and let His joy and freedom guide you in all you do.

III JOHN 4: "I have no greater joy, than to hear that my children walk in truth."

WEEK #21
SAY IT LIKE YOU MEAN IT

I remember when we raised our small children and wanted to teach them the importance of making amends after some sort of sibling squabble. The one determined to be chief offender would frequently be marched before he or she who was offended, and an apology was demanded: "Say that you are sorry!"... (no response)... Say "I'm sorry" right now! ... (still no response)... "Okay, you are going to seriously get it if you don't say 'I'm sorry' this very minute!"

Finally a begrudged response would come, and the mumbled and dejected "I'm sorry" would be offered up. Satisfied that I had "trained my little one up in the way he or she should go," I would return to my disrupted activity, congratulating myself on having instilled into my offspring the power of repentance...or not!

What we were really teaching was form and repetition. And in truth, there are many good habits that children learn from repetition, and from being told over and over what is the correct way to speak or look or talk to others. But if at some point this does not translate into a "heart" action, but remains only a reflex action (or a required action), the power of genuine repentance (a turning away from an error) will be lost. Genuine repentance opens the door for genuine forgiveness, and forgiveness offered and received is one of the most powerful tools for sustaining and developing a healthy marriage union.

But let us not get ahead of ourselves. We will speak of forgiveness in next week's devotional. Forgiveness is built upon an altar of repentance. When Jesus died, he offered the human race a powerful gift: turn away from a life of self will and self-serving, and turn to the Lordship of Jesus Christ. Surrender to the Savior, and in exchange the power of sin is broken from our lives, and we become completely free to relate to God as members of His family.

It is a great model for marriage. In order to have healthy relationship, these two interworking principles of "responsibility accepted and grace extended" must continuously flow as a functional dynamic between us.

But to get the ball rolling, we have to mean it...we really, really, have to mean it! We can't just run around saying "I'm sorry" as a technique we've learned in marriage manuals, because words spoken without full sincerity are worse than no words spoken at all. There is a tremendous power in "I'm sorry," but the power begins to be released when there is a true yearning in our heart to take accountability for anything we might have said or done to wound or pain this precious bond of marriage.

Why is it so difficult to both say it and mean it? Because it takes a serious measure of humility to go to anyone, and especially a spouse, and acknowledge that we have not fulfilled our call to love. If we walked in perfect love we would have perfect marriages. But our love remains imperfect, and so at times we wound one another with words, we hurt one another with our indifference. Sometimes we neglect, or are insensitive, or are simply preoccupied with our own internal battles. We are not there 24/7 as our loved one needs us to be. There may even be times when we are downright unfaithful, and the wounds of such can be brutal to bear, and even harder to repair.

Humility is the key. God gives grace to the humble. Grace is the power of God to carry out His purpose in our lives. Jesus was full of grace. We need more grace, and we need more Jesus in our homes. When we humble ourselves before our loved ones by admitting, sincerely, our error or our accountability for a conversation gone haywire, we are inviting in the grace of God. We are allowing Him to release His power upon us. And Oh how we need the power of God to sustain and elevate our homes! Without His power we are adrift, but so easily and willingly He will release that power to us.

There is a power, a grace, even to say "I'm sorry." There is an enabling of the Holy Spirit for us to step into the kind of humility that marriage requires. Let us admit in all honesty that we do not like to apologize. We do not like to make ourselves vulnerable before the one who knows us best. Our human pride wants to be right all the time. Yet even if we might be right, it is so liberating to take responsibility when a relationship has gone wrong. Isn't the preservation and vitality of the bond of far greater importance than self- justification? Do we really want to be "right" at the expense of our emotional intimacy and the joy of camaraderie?

Repentance, or accountability, or ownership over our error...these are all essential building blocks in a long haul marriage that becomes more of a pleasure with the passing of time. Hardened hearts coexist only in a state of misery. But a soft and humble spirit is a joy to live with.

So in summary, "say it like you mean it" and say it when you truly do mean it. With the personality of Jesus as your priority, you will discover the joy of meaning "it",

True humility brings great joy, and a great mantle of God's healing presence over your marriage relationship. Take responsibility, even if another will not. Your humility will release God's grace, and grace at some point becomes irresistible to even the most stubborn of hearts. Win one another over again and again with the unfailing meekness of our great King!

"He was wounded for our transgressions, He was bruised for our iniquities;
The chastisement for our peace was upon Him, and by His stripes we are healed.
He was oppressed and He was afflicted, yet He opened not His mouth; Isaiah 53: 5,7a

But He gives more grace. Therefore He says: "God resists the proud, but gives grace to the humble." "Humble yourselves in the sight of the Lord, and He will lift you up." James 4:6, 10

WEEK #22
ONE GOOD TURN DESERVES ANOTHER

Oh how wonderfully pleasant it is to be proven right! How grand for our enemy to grovel. How very much we savor that wonderful moment when one kneels before us, beseeching our mercy...that moment when we realize that the very fate of the one prostrate before us lies within our hands. It is a wicked pleasure, and one relished all too quickly. And, quite sadly, we are not usually exulting over an enemy in this scenario, but a very beloved family member or friend.

Here is an iron clad rule: those with whom we are closest will offend us most frequently. Therefore, in all likelihood, the most "offensive" person in your life will be the one you marry! What? Has this devotional detoured into madness? Not at all, and remember that when we say "offensive" we don't mean smelly, or ugly, or rude, or obnoxious; we are referring to the act of creating offense by acting toward another according to a standard that is less than the standard of God's perfect love.

The absence of love in a word, an action, or a look, will offend, hurt, or wound to some degree. You did not marry a perfect person. Your spouse will not, in your lifetime, become a perfect person. They will grow in love, but still from time to time miss the mark of love, and therefore, they will act in a manner that offends. And when they offend, Christ's command will compel them to eventually humble themselves and apologize.

And thus theoretically, if your spouse is walking in the true spirit of Jesus, they will be the one who apologizes to you more than any other person you will ever meet on this earth. You will hear the words "I'm sorry" a thousand times through the years, and then you will stop counting. It will become your culture, because you crave the culture of the kingdom.

But what will you do when the apology is laid at your feet? Will you extend the scepter of mercy, or will you hold grudges, steam for a week or more, withhold conversation, or simply embrace the deceiving impersonation of the balm of bitterness?

They have gone to great spiritual and emotional lengths to come to the point of true, humble penitence. Will you then be willing, in obedience to Christ, to forgive?

We have said that there are two essential components in the equation that releases the great power of God into a marriage. The first is to take responsibility when we have fallen short or failed. The second is to release grace when a failure has been recounted.

The power is in your hands, in many ways, of life and death. The life, or vitality, of your marriage bond is completely bound up in the principle of forgiveness. Likewise, we can release death, if we so tragically choose. Bitterness brings death. A hardened heart that won't release an offense keeps the offender in a place of agonizing bondage. And the relationship can never be normal or happy. We are stuck in neutral, and actually, we are stuck in reverse, until we complete the equation, and release a full measure of God's wonderful forgiveness.

Just as repentance takes humility, so also do we need the assistance of God to release full forgiveness. God's forgiveness is supernatural! It is not something we can toss about lightly. It goes in depth beyond our human understanding. It intersects with the Divine, and His presence floods a room each time it is extended. Godly forgiveness is more than a slap on the back or a peck on the cheek. It is more than a "never mind" or a "don't worry about it."

It is a radical wrenching open of the prison bars that have bound your loved one's soul. It is an alignment with the atmosphere of heaven. It is not easy for your flesh, for your flesh has been offended...perhaps grievously. But the Spirit of God who enables us to humble ourselves and seek mercy is the same Spirit who will enable us to rise beyond our bitterness and wounds, experiencing the joy that comes when we throw open the captive's cell and cry out to him to run freely into the open arms of God.

Yes, God's salvation and God's personality can be manifested in our homes. Our marriages can be an ongoing revelation of the Divine nature of our creator. All that Jesus released on the cross, you and I are able to appropriate and release into our marriage again and again. "Father, forgive him (or her) ...I know that they did not understand the pain that would cause me."

Sometimes we don't want to forgive. But in obedience to God's Word and pattern, we reach out and receive His power to extend grace. Sometimes we want our loved one to suffer for what they have done...perhaps to suffer our silence, or neglect, or withheld affection. But Jesus suffered on Calvary so that we would not have to experience the consequences of being a sinful people. When He is so willing to remove our judgment, why are we so willing to wish it upon others?

If one has come half way, acknowledging their error, let us respond in kind, and come the remainder of the way. Let us rebuild the bridge, discovering that the words "I forgive you" are even more compelling than the words "I'm sorry." Once spoken, the equation is complete.

The spiritual chemistry is set into motion, and a chemical bond is formed once again, stronger than ever before, for spiritual chemistry always supersedes natural chemistry. There are unbreakable laws in nature, and there are likewise unbreakable laws in the spirit realm: "He whom the Son sets free, is free indeed." "If we confess our sins, He IS faithful and just to forgive us..."; "there is now therefore NO condemnation to those who are in Christ Jesus."

One good turn deserves another. Walk in the power of grace extended. You will never regret having imitated your Savior in this most essential area of your married life.

"For if you forgive men their trespasses, your Heavenly Father will also forgive you." Matthew 6:14

WEEK #23
RUNNING BUDDIES

I used to run.

This is a shock to those who have only known me for a quarter century or less. But indeed it is true. Back in the earliest days of marriage, I would get up at 5:00 or 5:30 AM every morning and go running a loop around a lovely lake in our neighborhood. It had a well paved three mile path running the circumference.

My definition of success was anything under a 10 minute mile. So perhaps I should rephrase, and say that "I used to jog." I've never really been a runner, but even back in high school when I broke a seven minute mile, the thrill of moving faster than a brisk walk was always a worthwhile reward. I loved the adrenaline rush. I loved to daydream as I ran/jogged that I was training for the Olympics. And I especially loved running outdoors in the midst of nature's magnificence.

The trees around Rockland Lake were beautiful, and the swans on its still waters were magical. It should have been enough to fill any soul with contentment. But I have a problem, in that I am not a solitary creature. I don't like to eat alone, I don't like to be alone (for more than a few hours), and I don't like to exercise alone. I wanted a running buddy, but my best friend, my beloved wife, is neither a morning person nor a runner.

And so I did what is most likely the stupidest thing I have done relationally in my thirty two years of marriage: I asked two co-workers at my college kitchen job if they wanted to run with me. I knew they were runners. I knew they were early birds. And quite brainlessly, I also knew they were females...as in the opposite sex...and being a totally uninformed newlywed, I didn't see the slightest problem with running early each morning with a couple girls from work.

My guy friends weren't interested, so what difference would it make? Oh, the terrible naiveté of a twenty year old who hasn't been properly fathered or mentored. I hadn't a clue that this was a super dumb move on my part, until one day only one of the girls showed up. And the next day she showed up alone again. And by the 3rd or 4th time she showed up alone, driving with me to the quiet solitude of Rockland Lake, I slowly began to realize that I was potentially in a seriously idiotic situation.

One of those early mornings as we jogged around the track was what I would call (in retrospect) a "gracious intervention of God." We had stopped to catch our breath for a moment and enjoy the rising sun, when who should come running around the corner from the other direction, but none other than the most absolutely serious and stern Bible Professor of all the faculty on our campus.

He knew me, he knew that I was just married, and he knew that the girl I was jogging with was not my wife. He looked at me with the most penetrating "you are on the precipice of eternal damnation stare" that a scholarly sage could ever affix upon an ignorant young man. I was utterly mortified, and I was utterly awakened.

Like I said, "a gracious intervention of God." That was the end of my running career at Rockland Lake, and other than a damaged reputation before one who never mentioned a word (but only eyed me suspiciously in class), I had escaped the snare unscathed, and became a whole lot wiser.

We need a buddy in a great number of life's arenas, including the arena of physical fitness, but that buddy must never be someone of the opposite sex, unless we happen to be married to them. I've counseled young couples numerous times: "Buddy relationships with the opposite sex end the moment you are engaged to be married."

We cannot fool ourselves into thinking that we are spiritual enough to keep up with our old girlfriends or boyfriends from High School, to chit chat with our former heartthrobs from youth group, or to hang out with our co-workers who are across the gender aisle. Our intimacy, our friendship, our whispered confidences are now bound to the one from whom we will never part, and let us make sure to not carelessly lay the groundwork for a potential parting that we had never imagined possible.

There are some ways in which spouses are different and are not meant to be the same. Some will be night owls and some will be up with the birds. Some love to saunter and some prefer to sweat. But here is a challenge for any married couple: when it comes to the care of God's temple, your body, do everything in your power to find common ground and a common goal.

The body is a gift from God, a habitation for His Glory, and a wonderful vessel for living out our earthly destiny. It will get old, but it doesn't have to collapse into a tragic heap of neglect, layered cellulite, self-abuse through food intoxication, or general couch potato malaise. There is something wonderful and rewarding about maintaining our health and caring for our bodies.

But remember, the body is also the place of great sensuality and temptation. If one of us stays fit, while the other doesn't care, the fit one will suffer the loneliness of self-control, while the slothful will sulk with suspicion that their self-indulgence has sullied their appeal. In other words, "you don't love me because I'm fat...I'm old...I'm not good looking anymore!" These self-torturing words have driven many a fine family apart.

Make a determination together to take advantage of one of the best of our recent cultural trends, and that is the trend toward exercise, healthy eating, and a general focus on physical fitness. This was not the priority of previous generations, but today we hear a wake-up call from the Spirit of God to "be good stewards of the gift He has given, and to do our best to live long and live strong," all so that we can enjoy this life fully and stay active and available for all that He would require.

We might not all be marathoners, but we can all do our part to cheer one another on, and strive together to be the best that we can be in every arena of life. We can be our beloved's buddy in the things that really matter. And physical fitness matters, though not as much as prayer or Bible study, but nevertheless, it matters. It is important, and sharing it as a goal will strengthen your bond and keep you both charged up with that God-designed adrenalin high that He has created your body to enjoy and pursue.

"Physical exercise is of some value, but godliness is valuable in all areas of life, rewarding us in both this present life, and in the life that is to come." I Timothy 4:8

WEEK #24
THE POWER OF A PROMISE

There is an old fashioned phrase that was used to describe the reliability of a man's promise. A reliable man would confirm the safety of conducting business with him by saying "my word is my bond." In other words, he didn't have to put up a house or land or cattle as collateral to guarantee the deal - he only had to give his word. And his word was a guarantee, because that man was raised in an era when those of reputation followed through on their promises. They would rather face loss than break their bond.

Psalm 15 tells us that "the righteous man swears to his own hurt, and does not change." A man of character or integrity will maintain his vow or oath, even when it costs him dearly. He will not break his word. He will not change.

Today I've been pouring over the vows that my niece will exchange with her fiancé just 24 hours from now. I've been thinking much about vows. In the past, wedding vows were so sacred. It was a tragedy to break them, and many suffered great inconvenience and sometimes even personal heartache for the sake of maintaining vows they had made long ago.

People change and can be tough to live with, and all vows at some point become tested and placed under pressure. But in days gone by it was understood that such vows were made before God. They were made with God as a living witness. He was the One to whom we were making ourselves accountable. These promises were not to be easily broken.

Today we observe a tragic trend across Western cultures and nations...even in developing nations. Vows have become negotiable. Promises are thought to stay strong and be binding as long as the relationship or agreement is convenient and pleasing. But the moment discomfort or disappointment comes, people abandon without hesitation the promises previously made.

There is little conviction. There is little remorse. I would dare say this is reaching epidemic proportions. Numerous couples affiliated with the Christian faith are now saying they have "chosen to no longer be married...but simply to be friends." They declared the same vows on their wedding day as have so many other couples - but for them the promise was not a promise. The oversight and witness of God's Spirit was not a prevailing factor. They've broken their pledge, and then moved on with their lives without a care in the world.

What is the basis for this ease with which so many are walking away from publicly declared promises of fidelity, loyalty, devotion, and lifelong partnership?

I have a suspicion that all of this is rooted in a profound ignorance of the character of God. People do not understand how serious God is about our words. They don't understand how serious God is about His own words. There is something very particular about the character of God: He absolutely follows through on everything He says and promises. He never lies. He does not change.

The very heavens and earth could pass away, but His word would never be changed or broken. He is a promise maker, and a promise keeper. He is not afraid to commit, for He knows that He will absolutely follow through.

Marriage is a commitment, and the marriage vows are a public declaration that we are in this for the long haul. We are going to do this for life...this will in fact become our life! We are not experimenting. We are not testing the waters. We have been led by His Spirit, made up our minds, and there is no turning back. We are not afraid to promise because we intend to keep our word.

Why must we be so dramatic...so concrete in our declarations about marriage? It is for the very reason that we are called to be, and desire to be, like our Savior. Our commission is to imitate the Divine. We are not saved so that we can redefine the standard, but rather so we can be empowered to a higher place of grace than what the rest of the world has known. We become living reproductions of the personality, character, and vocalization of God. Christ lives in us, and the world sees there is a genuine hope for knowing God's glory.

People of faith do not understand that when they have bounced in and out of a contract, they have profoundly misrepresented God. They have allowed themselves a liberty that would terrify them if God granted it unto Himself.

Imagine if God told us, "I'm no longer in covenant with you, but I still have kind feelings for you." "I won't keep up my side of the relationship, and I can no longer secure your future or eternity, but I wish you the best of luck. No hard feelings." That thought is abhorrent.

We do not want such a God. The very thing that distinguishes our God is that such vacillation and changeability is unthinkable. Once He has pledged His love to us through His Son Jesus Christ, He is ours forever, and we likewise are His. He will not break His promise. He will never leave us or forsake us. He will not exchange us for another, or walk away because we've become difficult to live with. He keeps His word…forever.

If we understand the power of God's promise toward us, I believe that we in-turn are empowered and motivated to express the same level of devotion in our relationships with our fellow man, whether marriage, family, or friendship. Loyalty needs to come back in style. Our vows are holy because they are patterned after His personality. We are promise keepers because we are imprinted with the DNA of the greatest Promise Keeper who ever walked this planet.

Let us be people who take seriously our words. Let the world re-discover that the Christian community can be counted upon, that believing businessmen are the most reliable to deal with, and that faith based marriages do in fact have the foundations for permanence and success. Let us take back forcefully what the enemy of our souls is trying to steal from our generation. Let us follow His example once again.

"Not a word failed of any good thing which the Lord had spoken to the house of Israel. All came to pass" Joshua 21:45; "But as God is faithful, our word to you was not 'yes' and 'no'….for all the promises of God in Jesus Christ are Yes, and in Him Amen." II Corinthians 1:18-20

WEEK #25
DON'T BUY A CHEAP MATTRESS!

Here is an interesting statistic: the average American couple will spend between $10,000-$30,000 on their primary vehicle, (if bought new), and will occupy that vehicle for a daily average of less than 1 hour. That same couple will spend less than $1,000 on their bed, in which they will spend an average of 7-8 hours out of each 24 hour cycle. There is a compulsion toward excess comfort and image in our culture when it comes to vehicles; we tend to buy way beyond what is required. Many overspend for what is seldom used. It is a reflection of how much we are affected by style over substance.

But with beds, there is a compulsion toward penny pinching. The same couple that drools over the shiny "must have" in the dealer parking lot will drive from there to the discount mattress provider because, for some reason, we hate to spend money on beds and mattresses. After all, what neighbor is going to know? Who is going to be impressed? All we do is sleep in it anyway.

Exactly!

Approximately one third of your married life will be spent together in bed. There is no venue you will find where you will be consistently in such close proximity. Couples love a nice drive in the countryside together. It is quality time alone. But eight hours? That is way beyond a Sunday afternoon outing. That is serious space invasion. There is no escaping one another in bed. You are bound together by the blanket, confined by the comforter, shut in by the sheets (especially the ones that are tucked in at the bottom of the bed - whose idea was that anyway?).

Your sights and sounds and smells are all mixed together in one eight hour odyssey of dreaming, tossing, turning, blanket hoarding, hot flashes, frozen feet, long late night chats, and excess analysis of all those things we failed to accomplish in the preceding day. There are a few other things that beds are good for, but we might want to save that discussion for a later chapter.

All this leading us to the inescapable conclusion that your investment in a bed is one of the most important financial decisions you will make. Your physical health and rest alone is sufficient reason, married or unmarried, for a willingness to pamper yourself a bit in this one area. We are not talking about fancy woodwork here, but about a mattress, plain and simple, that will grant you sweet slumber and comfortable cuddling.

Our honeymoon bed was a real doozy. We were housed in a small village in rural Spain by a beloved Uncle who wanted to treat us to a "genuine" experience of rustic life. Not recommended for your honeymoon! The bed was perhaps 30-40 years old. The mattress bowed severely in the middle. True, we were honeymooners and wanted to be as close as possible, but forced proximity is never a good idea.

It was not possible to sleep on one side or the other. Both of us invariably rolled toward the middle, even when we tried to cling to the sides of the mattress with our fingernails, or tied our waists to the railings. It was impossible. For a full week we entered the bed on opposite sides, then gracefully rolled downhill until we met. Of course, we did not complain. We laughed, and meeting in the middle was our preferred course of action anyway.

But a good night's sleep was not to be had, even after a full day of touring and an evening of intimacy. We were madly in love, but our bed mocked us and warred against our desperate need for refreshing. Thirty plus years later we are still laughing, but we will NEVER again enter willingly into such a bed.

Someone once introduced us by saying "they are sold out missionaries, and don't care what kind of bed they sleep in!." I must decline this accolade. True, we have slept on concrete slabs, in jungle hammocks, on the ground, on plywood, on piled up blankets, and in beds two feet too short. We have done what we needed to do. But if a 5 star hotel mattress is offered, you better believe I will take it.

A good night's rest is critical for mental and physical function. And even if it wasn't, I'm in a better mood usually when I'm not in pain. Nothing like sinking sweetly in mattress heaven with the one you love after a long haul flight or a day of demanding responsibility at home.

I've been the mattress cheapskate in the past. We've bought everything else we didn't need and scrimped on the one item that is truly most important. But those days are over. Get a used car, but don't buy a used bed! Don't fall for the ads that promise "amazing comfort for only $99" - it doesn't exist. The bed is the locale of your greatest intimacy as husband and wife. It is your private escape. Your home may be a humble hamlet, but let your bed become your royal chamber. There the King and Queen of the castle reside, renewing their love and growing old gracefully together.

The Bible talks about beds. In fact, it endorses investing in a good bed! It tells us that "marriage is honorable, and the marriage bed is undefiled." (Hebrews 13:4) Well, maybe I am stretching my Biblical interpretation a bit here. But the point is made. That bed is your domain as husband and wife. It is your place of blessing and joyful union.

Go out and get yourselves a good mattress...and live happily ever after!

"And the Lord God caused a deep sleep to fall on Adam, and he slept." Genesis 2:21

(I think He might have laid him out on a really awesome mattress before performing the rib reduction surgery from which he created Eve) :)

WEEK #26
COME GROW OLD WITH ME
THE BEST IS YET TO BE!

Malachi 2:15 tells a man that he should *"not forsake the wife of his youth."* Why would a man abandon the wife of his youth? It is because he woke up one morning and discovered she had grown old. He had grown old as well, but being a selfish and soul-centered man, he decides that he is entitled to eternal youth in his partner, even though his own body is fading rapidly. He dumps her for a younger model, one who can fan the flames of his pride and physical desire.

The cultures of Western civilization have become obsessed with staying young. People are slicing up their faces faster than you can peel a mandarin orange. They are botoxing & detoxing on a regular basis. There is a fear of being eternally old, and so we have launched a quest to be eternally young.

There is little self-awareness of heaven, and so we try to carve out our permanence here on earth. It is a fool's errand, for this life is but a vapor, and the body was not designed to function forever.

We need to get our thinking straight on this matter, or our marriages, like so many before us, will suffer neglect and the disappointment that comes from unrealistic expectations.

What should we realistically expect when we say "I do?" Is personal satisfaction and physical gratification really the non-negotiable right of every tax paying Westerner? Why are people who have labored and loved together for 30 or 40 years suddenly calling it quits?

Let us first recognize that society does not value age and experience as much as the Scriptures do. In ancient Eastern societies, elderly people were revered and sought after. They were counselors and trusted analysts. They knew the ways of the world and the ways of men. But today they are often perceived quite the opposite.

The young see themselves as saddled with the care of the old, with budgets being drained by social safety nets that are increasingly consumed by the needs of the dependent. Older cultures and values are renounced. There is a strain of thinking that we are the enlightened generation. Our forefathers got it all wrong. They have nothing to contribute, and their values have been outgrown.

Imagine growing old in such a climate, where slowly but inexorably the people around you begin to ask the question, "what value are you to me?" Imagine if this creeps into our married life. We no longer see ourselves as living with a treasure of experience and shared history, but rather with one whose declining senses and non-Hollywood appearance makes partnership a chore, rather than a joyful triumph of many decades fought for and hard won.

Let us accept that "growing old" is a part of a normal human life. Gray hair and wrinkles are not curses, but signs of our survival and success. Let us recall the disposition of man, created by God to be comprised of body, soul, and spirit.

First things must be kept first, and the spirit of a man or woman is always the place where decisions must be made. Our spirit, where we commune with our creator, is that component of our human trinity which must insist on being in charge. It is there that covenants are made and kept. It is there that values are recognized and stood upon.

We cannot become slaves to the body. The body, with its desires and needs, is by no means evil, but it is also by no means ever intended to call the shots. Those who are led by the whims of the body will get every call wrong. They will "sell their soul" for a pot of porridge. They will judge their lover by the outward form, rather than by the inward beauty of a life dedicated to God.

And the soul is no more a friend in these matters than is the body. The soul, our realm of emotions and intellect, can search for that which promises consolation and rest, a relationship without bumps or inconsistencies, a love which gives everything but demands nothing in return. The soul, un-yielded to the influence of our enlightened spirit, can betray us in a heartbeat.

Our eyes lock with the eyes of one to whom we are not promised, and suddenly it seems that life cannot be endured without a new companion - the one we should have married in the beginning - the one who will renew our youth and restore our dignity - the one who bears a promise and a lie that, with them, we can recapture the vitality of years ago that seems to have been lost forever.

Man and woman of God, live in the realm of the Spirit and allow Him to make your own spirit Commander-in-Chief of your choices and desires. Renounce the lie, and embrace the blessing of a journey shared until the end. Laugh off the wrinkles and the humbling of advancing age. Love that countenance that greets you each morning, looking less like the glowing teenager from 60 years past, but more beautiful than ever internally after decades walked in the presence of God.

If you look closely enough, you will realize this internal beauty is indeed reflecting through the outward countenance. Beauty is in the eye of the beholder if you know what true beauty is, and if you know wherein it can be beheld.

There are treasures reserved for those who run this race until the end. There is a camaraderie and a shared joy that no one else can comprehend. It is one of life's foremost blessings, it waits for you and beckons you not to miss out on the glory of these closing chapters. Determine in your youth to meet seniority with open arms.

Don't fear it, don't run from it, don't denounce it. God has prepared it and designed it with its own special privileges and surprises. And oftentimes the experienced grace of God in the latter days far exceeds what we've known together in our younger days. Just ask Abraham and Sarah!

"Even youths can faint and become weary, and young men can fall, but those who wait upon the Lord shall renew their strength; they shall mount up with wings like eagles, they shall run and not be weary, they shall walk and not faint." Isaiah 40:31

WEEK #27
UNCLE HARRY AND AUNT SPITKISSY

Every family has them; those crazy relatives whose sole purpose in life seems to be the unending torment of all sane members of the family. Aunt Spitkissy was the nickname for an older aunt who used to greet us as kids with extreme affection - demonstrated by the deposit of her saliva which ran down our cheeks after she planted a big welcome kiss on us upon our arrival from a long road trip to her Appalachian home. None of us were too fond of Aunt Spitkissy and we developed well-honed avoidance skills over the years to aid us during arrival and departure. It was always a good time for an emergency bathroom visit!

Uncle Harry was another famous one. He would call in the middle of the night to tell of how his family had poisoned him. On one visit he stood up during the dinner hour and wrapped his huge farmer's hands around my neck from behind, then announced quite soberly that "with one squeeze, I could snap your head right off of your shoulders!" I calmly assured Uncle Harry that I believed him and that he was indeed a very strong man...and it would be really great if he returned to his place at the table and finished his hamburger so that he could retain that wonderful gift of potentially lethal human power.

Well, both Uncle Harry and Aunt Spitkissy are in Glory now. We assume they are in their right minds and have all their quirks straightened out, as heaven is no place for misplaced drooling or head severing shenanigans.

Not all families have crazy uncles and slobbering elderly aunties, but every family has someone that gives cause to cringe on occasion. They blunder their way through life, and the wake of their created waves seems to constantly be washing against the doors of our castle, threatening our serenity and demanding that we be dragged into their messes again and again. They may be unstable, addicted, socially awkward, self-obsessed, hypochondriac, kleptomaniac, nervous talkers, personal bubble violators, bi-polar, aromatically challenged...or just undefinably but undeniably weird!

Oh what to do with these strange and odd appendages to our attempts at living a normal life? There IS something that must be done. Those who are unstable or living on the outer fringes of normal human behavior seem to have in common a need to "invade" the orderly world of responsible living. They will not hide in corners, but will assert themselves loudly at each family gathering. They will ring your phone at all the wrong times, and will demand that you bail them out each time they have created another mess of their own choosing.

We cannot simply throw them away because they are offensive and inconvenient. God seems to have a special place in His heart for these impossible cases. They provide us golden opportunities to mine the depths of the Spirit principles of patience, kindness, goodness, and love. But giving them the privilege of uncensored or unrestrained behavior is not an act of charity, nor is it sustainable in our own orderly lives. Our sanity will be strained, and our own marriage relationship can even suffer. Guilt for the sufferings of the simple-minded can begin to drive us, and a home steered by guilt will crash very swiftly upon rocky shores.

People say that when you "marry an individual, you have married their family." Not true. When you have married an individual, you have inherited a degree of responsibility for their family. But your covenant with the clan is not the same as your covenant with one another. You must protect the sanctity of your home.

The Uncle Harrys and Aunt Spitkissys of the world will forever be with us, but here are a few tips for managing their attempts at invasion:

- <u>Never try to play the role of God.</u> We cannot save anyone in our family. We are not meant to die for their deliverance. Only One could pay that price, and He already paid it upon the Cross. It is up to our loved one to take advantage of the grace that is freely offered there...or not. If they don't receive God's grace and power for personal change and transformation, we cannot force it upon them.

- <u>Set absolute boundaries and hold to them.</u> Genuine love is always firm. The main problem of the unstable is that they are infuriated by boundaries. They want the world to grant them free reign to do as they please. They are preoccupied with their own rights, but oblivious to the rights of others. People may NOT do whatever they want in your home and in front of your children. You set the rules...and they can choose to abide by them...or to lose the privilege of your hospitality.

- <u>Speak the truth in love</u>. The Bible teaches us that "the truth shall set men free." Jesus as well refers to Himself as "The Truth." We don't help people by avoiding the obvious, or by coming up with inoffensive terms for what everyone knows is really just plain old sin (actions contrary to the word, will, and character of God)! Whether or not they embrace the truth, we at least owe them the chance to make that decision.

"But you, beloved, building yourselves up on your most holy faith, praying in the Holy Spirit, keep yourselves in the love of God, looking for the mercy of our Lord Jesus Christ unto eternal life. And on some have compassion, recognizing their unique situation; but others save with fear, pulling them out of the fire, hating everything that is polluted by the sinful behavior of man's fallen nature." Jude 1:20-23

WEEK #28
WE WALK BY FAITH, NOT BY FEELING

Marriage is a huge undertaking. Successful marriages are years in the making. Those who pass the 10 year mark have already faced and conquered some sizable challenges. They've long ago learned that for a Christian marriage to work, we have to understand the Biblical teaching on faith.

Faith is central to our marital happiness. Not the faith defined only by our belief in God or our belief in Jesus, but faith as defined by our practical willingness to live and love one day at a time. We must be confident that this formula of faithfulness given to us by God will eventually bring about a series of desired results in our relationship.

For example, our weaknesses will not disappear overnight. We may have to endure a long period of time as our spouse works through their issues with God. And they, as well, may have to endure with our process. Faith believes that love never fails. Faith in God means that I have confidence that covenant is worth keeping. I believe by faith that the grass is never greener on the other side. I refuse the whispers that come from time to time that I can find a deeper happiness with another.

The crisis in marital fidelity today is a crisis of faith. Individuals have little conviction that it "pays to do right." They move by their feelings, and feelings ungoverned by God's Word can be among the most traitorous of all our impulses.

Faith always hears the voice of God. In fact, we cannot live by faith without knowing and receiving God's Word. "Faith comes by hearing, and hearing by the word of God" (Romans 10:17). Many have replaced God's voice with the voice of their emotions and desires. But our fragile flesh is untrustworthy. Couples need to be grounded in God's Word, listening to preaching and teaching, meditating upon it in private devotion, and sharing it together in conversation. The less "Word" in our homes, the weaker our capacity for faith...and faith must be maintained if we are to outlast the storms.

Faith always believes. God speaks great things about your spouse. Do you believe it? When the Bible calls you both a son or a daughter of God, do you believe it? I have to believe what God says not only about me, but equally about my partner. When the word of God declares that we are forgiven, do I believe that regarding my spouse's most recent offenses? We have watched some hold their husband's or wife's failure over their heads for years. This is not faith. This is unbelief in the power of God to forgive, and to cleanse us from all unrighteousness.

Faith trusts. When change is slow in coming, do I trust in the faithfulness of God? If He has given us promises regarding our relationships, provision, or future, do we throw in the towel because He didn't come through in the time frame that we demanded? Faith trusts that God is always working, and that He hears and answers our prayers.

<u>Faith acts with eager expectation.</u> It expects results. When I serve my spouse out of legalism or obligation, there is no joy and often no reward. But when I obey the word out of faith in God, there is a liberty in submission and service. It is not what I <u>have</u> to do because I'm a Christian, but it is what I am <u>privileged</u> to do, with the joy of knowing that faith based actions always bring down the grace of God.

Remember, grace is power. We need God's power in our homes, and faith is the key to unlocking the power (grace) of God. Romans 5 tells us that *"through Jesus Christ, we have access by faith into this grace in which we stand, and thus rejoice in the hope of the glory of God."* Faith is ready to act because faith knows that power will come.

By faith I can bless those I love without fear I'll be taken advantage of or left looking like an unappreciated fool. My service and my humility bring God's enabling and His solution to every challenge we face. Faith will always express your profession of love through concrete action.

<u>Faith even knows!</u> Faith knows that it will get an answer from God. Faith knows that God's word, applied to our homes, works every time. Faith knows that righteousness is the right choice and that it will be rewarded. Faith knows that God hears and answers prayer. Faith knows that God is there and He will meet us in our time of need. Faith never crosses its fingers, but faith raises its hands in celebration before the parting of the clouds.

Galatians 5:6 tells us that *"the only thing which produces lasting value in our relationship with Jesus Christ is faith working through love."* These two are the dynamic duo between us and God, and they are the same between husband and wife. It is one thing to love you, but when that love is an extension of my faith walk with

God, then there is an entirely new dimension and power to that love. Imagine releasing the power of God upon one another in a marriage relationship! The more I believe, the more effectively I can love. The more I trust in God, act upon His word, and have confidence in the outcome, the more freely my love will flow.

Young couples today are being sold a lie leading them to believe that pleasure and feeling are the truest barometers of marital health and fulfillment. Don't sell yourselves short. Pleasure and feeling have great value, but it is what we believe about God and His Word when we are down in the trenches of life that will define our long term joy in marriage. This is your great gift to your beloved - your faith in the faithfulness of God!

"At the end the vision will speak, and it will not lie. Though it's coming seems delayed, wait for it; because it will surely come, it will not be delayed. The just shall live by his faith." Habakkuk 2:3-4

WEEK #29
PAINT THE FRONT DOOR RED

I've never been much one for the sight of blood. Some people like to watch the immunization needle go into their arm - I'd just as well look away. Not that I'm the fainting type, but I figure I've only got so much of the red stuff; I don't really appreciate them taking out five vials at a time to check cholesterol levels, prostate specific antigens, sugar, uric acid, triglycerides, testosterone, ...and the list goes on. I suppose they have to shed a bit of my blood to make sure that I am healthy on the inside.

I always feel sort of sorry for the people of George Washington's day. Back then there were crazy medical theories about "bleeding" people who had illness, with the idea that somehow a good blood loss would resolve whatever infection was raging through their bodies. Whether malaria, yellow fever, or just some unknown malady, a good doctor would slice and dice until his patient was good and pale. Somehow this was supposed to make them feel better.

Old George's doctor bled him a good number of times while on his deathbed...pretty much ensuring that it was actually his deathbed. Come to think of it, maybe I shouldn't mind those five vials being extracted after all. At least it comes out neatly through a sterile plastic tube and not some gash across my skull or upper arm.

Are your stomachs queasy yet? Yes, blood is not a pleasant topic of conversation. I watched my grandmother's maid in Damascus, Syria bleed out a lamb before roasting it for our dinner when I was 10 years old. My siblings and I completely lost our appetites. "Mary had a little lamb" and we did not appreciate that little lamb ending up on our supper plates the day after we had been petting it.

Strangely enough, however, blood is actually a vital ingredient in a happily married household. It sure enough was vital back in the day when the Israelites were being rescued from Egypt. A plague was to pass through the land, bringing death upon the firstborn in every household. But God wanted protection for His own people, and so He instructed them to put the blood of a lamb on the doorposts and entry way of each home. That blood would be a sign that a covenant people were inside, and they were not to be harmed. God said to them *"Now the blood shall be a sign for you on the houses where you are. And when I see the blood, I will pass over you; and the plague shall not be on you to destroy you when I strike the land of Egypt."* (Exodus 12:13)

We are also told in the Scriptures that "without the shedding of blood, there is no forgiveness of sin." Back in the Old Testament they were totally dependent on repeatedly bleeding out cows and sheep for sacrifices. But judgment was always lurking, as sin always repeats itself.

There aren't enough animals in the whole world to deal with mankind's innumerable offenses. But thankfully, God intervened, sending His only Son Jesus to bleed and die, so that we could be forgiven once and for all - permanently, forever, never again to be in danger of judgment. It was the most profound bloodletting in earth's history.

It was ugly and gory. It was painful. But it brought about the most profound level of health that men can know. It repaired the breach between us and God. It offered permanent purification of the heart. It crushed the power of darkness, fear, and condemnation. And for those who believed, it forever painted the doorways of their hearts red, free from all threats of judgment and death. Security became their portion, the ability to sleep well at night, because in spite of what was wreaking havoc outside their walls, the grace of God was prevailing within.

It gives me a whole new perspective on blood.

And so the challenge for husband and wife is to keep the doorway of their home and hearts painted red, the color that repels judgment and condemnation, for indeed we who repeatedly err and offend one another are in desperate need of a permanent declaration of righteousness. For the destroyer will in-fact attempt, again and again, to barge through the doors of our relationship, hurling accusation, cursing with condemnation, and tempting us to deprive one another of that very promise which Jesus died to provide: His security.

We can have the knowledge that we are once and for all washed in the blood of the Lamb of Calvary. This is a precious treasure and also a potent weapon of defense. The specter of death and judgment may not enter. We have been painted permanently in the color of His sacrifice.

Sometimes a human venting of anger is referred to as "seeing red." I would urge you to see red from a very different point of view. Not the venting of rage, but the wall that stops rage in its tracks. A heart painted red is one where the enemy of our soul is halted. A marriage painted red is a place of peace, where we are long-suffering with each other's weakness because we know that the King of Kings Himself is in residence within our hearts.

When we are tempted to see one another through the lens of disappointment or frustration, we will pause, readjust our rose-colored glasses, and see yet again as He sees. We will see the righteous, blood-washed, sanctified, and deeply loved human being that God has granted us the privilege of walking with through this life. We will see a Savior guarding their heart, reminding us that judgment, even our own, dare not enter. No one is qualified or entitled to violate His decree. It is best to embrace the blood that speaks volumes and pass one more night in peace.

"For if the blood of bulls and goats and the ashes of a heifer, sprinkling the unclean, sanctifies for the purifying of the flesh, how much more shall the blood of Christ, who through the eternal Spirit offered Himself without spot to God, cleanse your conscience from dead works to serve the living God?....therefore brothers, having boldness to enter the Holiest by the blood of Jesus, by a new and living way which He consecrated for us, through the veil, that is His flesh, and having a High Priest over the house of God, let us draw near with a true heart and full assurance of faith....and let us consider one another in order to stir up love and good works." Hebrews 9:13,14 / 10:19-24

WEEK #30
SILLY PUTTY

Are you too young to remember this? Silly Putty used to be the ultimate Christmas gift when we were kids. In fact, if a Christmas went by and there was not Silly Putty in the stocking, then it really wasn't much of a Christmas. With our fresh egg full of Silly Putty, we joyfully would open up the colorful Sunday comics in the newspaper and skillfully press down our delicious smelling Silly Putty and voila!... up came an exact copy of the comic imprinted upon the Silly Putty! Wonder of wonders, the precise images of Dagwood and Marmaduke and Archie would be preserved on our Silly Putty to be gazed upon forever...or at least until we crumpled up the Silly Putty and imprinted yet another Mona Lisa masterpiece of the comic world on it.

When we tired of this copying game, we eventually chewed up the Silly Putty, as the taste was palatable, and you could make a really cool popping noise between your teeth. But newsprint is not really meant for human consumption. Average lifespan of a container of Silly Putty...about six hours. End of Christmas.

But now in adulthood, we discover that Silly Putty continues to reign. It reigns through the efforts of others who want to imprint everything around them so that it comes up looking exactly like themselves. They are the silly putty wanting to make you into their own image. They know what's best for your marriage, how you should relate, what you should spend your money on, and so on and so forth.

Churches can even move improperly into this direction, and rather than teaching us how to grow uniquely in the Holy Spirit, they simply want to impose the 'Jesus way of life' upon you according to their idea of how it should be lived out. Often unintentional, but they can easily steal your uniqueness as a couple and try to turn you into a clone of their ministry or life philosophy.

Let me encourage you to find your uniqueness, as a couple, in God. When you joined together something new was created that the world had never before seen. There is actually NO couple on planet earth exactly like the two of you! The "one flesh" that you have become is a new and previously undiscovered creation. It existed in theory as you courted and dated and engaged, and even pre-existed in the mind of God, but the theory became reality only after you exchanged your vows and launched into the unknown. You were born into a new life to be something unique in God.

You are able to impact the world around you in a way no one else can. You, as a couple, are able to reveal Jesus in a unique fashion, that no one else has ever been able to do. Why? Because no one else has ever been the two of you. Your union is a unique gift from God to the human race.

The mystery of Christ's bond with His church can be revealed through your bond with a slant never before seen. Something of His love and His humility and His service will uniquely reach people that will see His grace in a new way. And just maybe for the first time through who He creates YOU to be.

The challenge is to embrace that destiny of discovery. Life in God is anything but mundane. So many have missed the thrill of the chase, the exhilaration of pursuing His purpose and growing from glory to glory as new adventures unfold. Don't let human expectations box you in! Don't let the pressures of conformity keep you from the higher reaches of royalty. You ARE royalty. You are a son and daughter of God, and you ought not, you must not, you cannot live captive to the lesser master of peer pressure. Do not give anyone the smug self-satisfaction of seeing you in their own image, rather than the image of God.

Be yourselves! Find out who that unique, united self is in His image; no one else's. If there is to be any putty or imprinting power upon your life, let it be the Word of God applied firmly, to make you into a carbon copy of the Jesus whom the Holy Spirit reveals to you and through you.

Marriage manuals and conferences and workbooks are all well and good...even a 40 week devotional might be helpful now and then! But at the end of the day, the only affirmation that counts is that of the One who paid the price for the privilege of imprinting you with His own precious blood. He alone can seal you and write a permanent name upon your soul.

Don't run another man's race, and don't try to live out another couple's marriage. You are uniquely and beautifully created. Let the world see that beauty of Jesus shining through His creation as you walk in freedom to become whomever God joined you together to be.

"As for me, I will see Your face in righteousness; I shall be satisfied when I awake in Your likeness." Psalm 17:15

WEEK #31
LET FREEDOM RING

Today is July 4th, 2014, America's 238th birthday! I have a vivid memory of the 200th anniversary. In 1976 I was living in Trotwood, Ohio, and can recall President Gerald Ford instructing all "good" Americans to ring whatever bells they could at noon on that day in celebration of America's freedom. I was 13 at the time, and we had an old brass bell that hung over the stone well/dog house where my faithful hound Cookie resided.

Being a patriotic teen, I took the President's admonition quite seriously, and at noon sharp I went outside and rang that bell like the whole town was on fire. No one else was around, and I really can't recall whether I heard any other bells ringing or not. But "God bless America" I was going to ring that bell! Cookie gazed up at me from her rest with a look of disgust, as I finally spent myself on bell ringing and decided to head back into the house for some lemonade. I was confident that President Ford would be proud!

Freedom is an amazing thing, and America is an amazing country. It is a huge privilege to have been born in this nation, where women are not subjugated behind a veil, children are protected from child slavery and no one's 5 year-old is working all day in a sweat shop. It is amazing to be able to drive from one end of this vast nation to the other, and never once have to show a passport, religious I.D., or transit papers. It is incredible to enter a church freely and to worship without fear of arrest.

We have all these because 238 years ago people died to secure this freedom. Men of character spent months and years hammering out a Constitution that would secure individual rights and liberty. There is no doubt this nation was birthed in the plans and purposes of God; for God is a God of freedom, individual choice, and liberty. He Himself knows what it means to die to purchase this valuable commodity - the worthiest of causes...our salvation. In the Kingdom of God, Freedom is everything. Jesus said "he whom the Son sets free is free indeed!"

Our homes ought to have an overtone of that pure freedom offered by Jesus Christ. Even as we celebrate our privilege to live in this nation, we recognize that those very freedoms we've taken for granted are now under assault. Religious freedom in particular is no longer a guarantee. You are welcome and accepted IF you buy into a liberal government's view of what is acceptable conviction. Embrace a Biblical morality and you now are a threat to social order and peace, and are even threatened with bankrupting fines, business isolation, and in some extreme cases, even imprisonment.

Perhaps you may not be able to effectively influence or control what is going on in the larger sphere of your nation, but you most certainly can influence and control what goes on in your home. Will your home be free? Will it be a place of liberty, where individual uniqueness and conviction are welcomed? Or will it be a place where distinction and opinion bring rejection and withheld affection?

Will our children be mandated to clone themselves into our image? Will we recognize their unique calling and gifting in God? Will we embrace their personalities even though they may be different from our own? Will we encourage their desires as they enter adulthood to experience the exhilaration of personal choice as free agents living in free relationship with their creator?

So many religious homes are tragically just glorified prisons. We talk the talk and appear to walk the walk, but those close to us live in dread for fear of disapproval and censure if they don't tow the company line. The family image must be upheld. The rules as we've defined them cannot ever be reconsidered. It is, in such places, sometimes near impossible to even breathe!

But Jesus, appearing to his bewildered and terrified disciples after His resurrection, had one thing in mind: to restore their ability to breathe freely. They were paralyzed by failure and shame. They were imprisoned by their own guilt. And so He breathed on them, and said "peace to you...receive the Holy Spirit." Oh, the wonderful wind of freedom! How absolutely liberating in that moment to know all was well between them and the Heavenly Father.

Husband and wife, let the winds of the Spirit of God blow continually in your home. Let an atmosphere of grace be absolutely in control of every day and every conversation. Invite uniqueness and distinction. Be willing to have constructive conversation and to entertain honest questions. We have such a fear of letting one another "think." I mean, "what if they come up with a conclusion different than my own?" And so we structure out that possibility by predetermining each family member's preferences and perspectives. When they align with ours, favor is lavished. But God have mercy if they dare to think on their own. Is this really what we want to be or become?

May you find absolute joy, man and woman of God, in being transparent and open with one another. May your children grow up in an atmosphere that welcomes, and lays the foundation for, a lifetime of sweet fellowship and relaxed living. Let domination and consternation be banished. Listen well. Release one another fully to run after God and worship Him each in their own unique manner. And remind yourself that someone paid a high price to ensure that everyone's freedom is secure. Let's give Him, and one another, what He died for.

"Stand firm therefore in the liberty by which Christ has made us free, and do not be tied up again with a yoke of bondage" (to rules made up by men). Galatians 5:1

WEEK #32
CONGRATULATIONS!
YOUR MEMBERSHIP HAS BEEN RENEWED

A few days ago I sat with a man who told me that he was absolutely done with the "church world." He said "I never want to walk through the door again! I'm fed up with people...with politics...with gossip. I'm done...FINISHED! I'll just meet in a small home group from now on and save myself a lot of headache."

Pretty awful, huh? I mean, what an unbiblical, bitter, misdirected attitude, and I can totally relate! I was in the same place about six months back. I'm a preacher, a pastor, and lots of other roles in the midst of this collection of people we refer to as the "church." And I've been fed up, disgusted, and ready to throw in the towel on more than one occasion. Not proud of it, but the temptation comes to all.

Churches are full of imperfect people, betrayal, and intrigue. They are also full of a whole lot of wonderful things that we simply will not find anywhere else. Not talking about the church building here, but about the atmosphere created when God's family gets together to worship, learn, serve, and love. But many times the bad seems to outweigh the good, and the reexamination begins: "Do we really need to go to a church?." "Does it matter for our family or future?"

And wait a minute, but isn't this a marriage devotional? Why are we talking about the church? A good question, and I'm glad you asked!

The church has <u>everything</u> to do with marriage. In Ephesians 5 the Apostle Paul gives us a set of instructions to husbands and wives. Lots of good stuff in there about sacrificial service and a life of humility toward one another - but at the end of the sermonette he tells us that "he is talking about Christ and the church." His whole teaching on proper function and heart between husband and wife is actually a revelation, or a picture, of the relationship that Jesus has with His redeemed people; a people that the Bible refers to as "the church."

Is this all that important? Well, consider that today many are not only re-examining the role of the church, including church structure and government and leadership, but whole movements of Christian people are rejecting the concept altogether. They believe there is no longer room for the organizational church. They renounce buildings, elders, service order, and even their own need to belong. They are going to tough it out alone with Jesus, or catch a few minutes of 'drive through church' on the television Sunday morning. And they are not only greatly in error, but they are depriving themselves and their families of one of the essential components for healthy domestic life.

God did not design us to live in isolation. He created us to grow best in community. And the "church world," or the local gatherings of God's people, is absolutely the very best community we can ever belong to. And here is the funny thing: we don't sign up!

When we are born again, we are automatically signed up. We may not even believe in "membership," technically, but like it or not, we are in fact members of the body of Christ. Our family has just increased exponentially. We have more brothers and sisters than we would ever want.

We go from the challenges of our home, to the challenges of everyone's home. Everyone's joy, and everyone's sorrow suddenly becomes a part of our world. Sometimes it's awesome...and sometimes it stinks! But once we marry Christ, then like it or not, we have married into His extended family. And this membership package comes with a load of perks and benefits.

Here is why, very practically, every husband and wife need to be a part of a dynamic, local body of believers; one with sound teaching, structure, freedom, and Godly leadership. We need people around us who know more than what we know. Someone in that church will value, cherish, and know more than we do about marriage. Church is a place where marriage is still honored with its Biblical value. People fight for marriage in the kingdom of God. We need fighters around us, who will cheer us on and fight for us.

We need people who have run that race and learned how to work through the very same problems we are facing. We need seasoned counselors, veteran husbands and wives, who can declare with confidence that "God will make a way."

We need people in our lives who know how to pray. Families, ALL families, face challenges that are bigger than themselves. We need a place where we can share our struggles and have amazing people stand in prayer on our behalf before a loving God. We need people who will believe for us, in us, and with us.

We need a company of faith-filled friends. Successful marriage takes faith in God! The Scriptures tell us not to neglect gathering together with those of similar faith. Why? Because we need their faith to impact ours and lift us up to a higher level in our walk with God.

We need a place where our children can find identity with other children who are learning to love Jesus. A place where our children can sing and rejoice with kids their own age.

We need an atmosphere of corporate worship. God ministers to our lives and relationships in powerful ways during times of worship from His people.

We need Pastors and Elders in our lives. Leaders who love us and take seriously the fact that they are charged by God with looking out for our souls. Our marriage cannot become a completely private and secret journey. With wise and loving people watching out for us, we can avoid many of the pitfalls that have brought others to dissolution.

We need, as a husband and wife, a place where we can joyfully invest tithes and offerings. A local church provides us with the opportunity to be accountable and consistent.

We need a place where we can regularly be taught and grow together in the Scriptures. Our marriages will never outgrow this. When we discover revelation together of God's wonderful plan for our hearts and lives, it keeps the adventure alive. The world talks about restoring the spark to our romance and marriage. There is no greater spark than that of our spirit coming alive in the presence of God and in the thrill of discovering His truth for our lives.

No doubt about it - church has everything to do with successful marriage. We cannot go it alone. We not only need the body of

Christ, but we need to love the body of Christ. It is a phenomenal gift, the greatest collection of people on earth to which anyone can belong. It's membership is elite, vetted, and thoroughly approved by God. The price for membership was exorbitant - it's founder paid with His life so that we could join.

Seems sort of shortsighted to write off the church. A whole lot of energy was invested in getting us into it in the first place.

God has a church family for every married couple and family. We don't fit just anywhere, but there is somewhere that the Holy Spirit wants to fit us in as both "gift to" and "beneficiary of" the people of God. Make the selection of that people one of the highest priorities of your journey together.

"Now you are the body of Christ, and members individually." *I Corinthians 12:27*

"And He is the head of the body, the church..." *Colossians 1:18*

"So we, being many, are one body, and individually members of one another." Romans 12:5

WEEK #33
WHO NAMED THE HIPPOPOTAMUS?

The book of Genesis tells us two things early on about Adam. First, he had a responsibility to name every living creature that God had created, and second, that it was not good for him to be alone in his work. The work became somewhat unending, we might imagine, and so God put him to sleep and created a woman, a helper, out of his rib bone. The first thing Adam did was take one look at her and decree that her name was "woman." "I am man, you came from my flesh, therefore you shall be woman."

It sounds a bit caveman-like...but I'm sure there was some appreciation and perhaps even a tinge of romance in Adam's declaration.

These two stories of naming, both the animals and Eve, seem to run somewhat together and to be intertwined in Genesis Chapter 2. We are not certain that Adam had completed his assignment to name every single animal by the time Eve came on the scene. She entered the world and the biggest thing happening was Adam was on something like name number 68,345...and counting!

I'm not sure what language he spoke, or how God even taught him language since there was no one else to talk to. But obviously they were taught, and Eve came on the scene speaking the same lingo. I'm thinking she jumped right into her task, and I'm guessing even more that she might have rolled her eyes a bit at some of Adam's linguistic concoctions.

Men can at times be tediously pragmatic. What matters is getting the job done. We don't need frills or borders, matching napkins or atmosphere. I can just hear Adam saying "NEXT" as the animals filed by one by one. How many random letter arrangements can you manufacture in order to name every creature God created?

I'm quite sure he could not have completed this job on his own, and I'm quite sure that God looked down upon him as he worked his way through his checklist and thought: "We've got to get some help for this guy... It is most definitely NOT good for him to be alone; better get working on a partner who has a few qualities that this gardener seems to be lacking."

So when the hippo rolled around, I'm betting that Adam took a look at him and thought the only appropriate name was PIG! A big, fat, mud sloshing pig. Plain and simple. Short and to the point. We will call this monster of a porker a Pig.

Eve wasn't buying it. "Adam, what in the world? That is the most uncreative thought you've uttered all day! Where is your creativity and enthusiasm? This magnificent creature ought surely to utilize a maximum number of vowels and consonants. This behemoth needs a name befitting its monstrousness. You can't just call him a PIG!"

Now Eve is not out of line here. She sees angles and carries insights that this worn out zoologist might have lost perspective on about 40,000 animals earlier. She was made from him, but vested with gifts different than his. She was, after all, made to be his helper. She had the right to voice her thoughts and opinions on those tens of thousands of choices Adam was making.

His brain doesn't want to spend another minute thinking, but Eve is interested in more than just watering the garden and corralling the creatures. She is arranging flowers, redecorating the bedroom, and coming up with a myriad of cute nicknames for their furry friends. An utter and complete waste of time (from the man's point of view). But God did not leave him alone with his point of view. God inserted a helper, to talk things through, see things differently, and come to some creative conclusions together.

I'm thinking that Adam may have worked hard to bite his lip the first time Eve dared to suggest a name change. This came as a surprise. "Wasn't she created to take orders and simplify my life? Isn't she just supposed to do what I tell her or what I ask...no questions asked?" "Who asked her opinion anyway?" Poor Adam.

All human beings have a tendency to want the world around them to cooperate with their program. We want everyone to think about and see the world as we do. We agonize over diversity, refusing to grasp that these distinctions are not our enemy, but our friends. We are sure our job would run more smoothly if our co-laborers adopted our methods, but we are born incapable of seeing or knowing fully on our own.

I don't think Adam was ever going to finish his assignment solo. I think there is even a chance he would have misnamed the hippopotamus if Eve had not come along. He needed her second set of eyes. He needed to empower her to partner with him in the process of choosing, deciding, and then celebrating the results.

So many of us are just expected to not make waves, and to keep the peace by blindly adopting the program of another. But let us discover the creative power of naming and creating together. Loads of decisions must be made in life. Babies are named, homes and cars are purchased, diets are decided, and money is invested. No Christian home will thrive with Napoleon as Captain of the ship.

Dictators will always demoralize. Eve will keep us on an even keel, and even help release within us the resource to plow forward in our commission with a fresh gleam and passion. She is not a drag on our project performance, but a rudder that frequently turns us back toward the essence of our purpose.

Is she perfect and without the need of assistance herself? Is Adam the dolt that modern society often projects him to be? A resounding NO to both questions. Eve, too, needs help. She needs a man that will do more than stand idly by when she is about to make the worst choice of her existence, like listening to the seductions of a serpent who would tell her there is more to life than what this task-driven man can offer.

Her hero was there, watching in horror as she reached for the forbidden fruit, but he didn't stop her, intervene, or protest. He was her helper, or meant to be, just as she was his. They both had extraordinary contributions to make. They both could empower the other to maximum success. Both with freedom, both with value, but both needing the support of a grateful partner.

Let us not strain at gnats. Let's not fight over who names what. Let us learn to defer and to delight ourselves in our loved ones' diversity. It must have taken some getting used to, this new partnership between man and woman for Adam and Eve. I don't think they woke up and hit the ground running. They had to learn how to communicate, how to work together, how to love, and how to grow a garden. They must have (sometimes) shaken their heads, whispering to God behind the Fig tree, "I just don't understand him," or "I just don't get her at all!."

But they persevered, (even through tragic mistakes), gave birth to sons and daughters, became the father and mother of mankind, and launched the God plan of populating the earth with a line that would one day become His very own family. They didn't get it perfect, but they got some things right.

In the end, it doesn't really matter who got to name the hippopotamus. What mattered in the end was that they stuck together, and they learned to live and love. They must have been a marvelous sight in their ancient years, giggling over petty disagreements long gone by and sighing in wonder at the amazing grace of God that had kept them for so long.

"Who then is Paul, and who is Apollos, but ministers through whom you believed, as the Lord gave to each one? 'I planted, Apollos watered, but God gave the increase'. So then neither he who plants is anything, nor he who waters, but God who gives the increase. Now he who plants and he who waters are one, and each one will receive his own reward, according to his own labor. For we are God's fellow workers." I Corinthians 3:5-9

WEEK #34
TECHNO ALIEN INVASION

This devotional topic would have been unthinkable 30 years ago. Way back then, in the paleolithic neanderthal age of instrumentation, we did not even have the concept of a personal cell phone in every pocket, let alone a smart phone.

In college we "typed" our papers, and were especially excited to have a typewriter with a self-correcting ribbon. I still think that I am typing on my computer. It became "keyboarding" some years back, but my brain cannot adapt to that terminology. Miss Mavis told me in the 7th grade that what I am doing is typing, and I'm quite sure that Miss Mavis was correct.

We were very excited as newlyweds to hook up our home telephone back in 1983. It was a handy dandy $12.95 model that boasted push button numbers. But of course we were not prepared for the siren sounds of the fast advancing tech invasion, so when the phone rang loudly in the middle of the night, a most unnatural sound, we began to shout and panic as to how we should manage this frontal wave assault on our sanity.

Holding the evil device in my hands, I could find no way to stop its eardrum piercing ring, and so I gingerly lifted the phone from its cradle. An eerie silence descended upon our bedroom. Fearful that it would revive and again attack our sleep, I ripped it out of the wall, cord and all. It seemed dead enough, and so we entered back into the blissfully silent world of chirping crickets, distant bullfrogs, and a lone train whistle echoing through the night. It was a long, long time ago...

Fast forward to today, where the alien invasion is firmly entrenched. It has attached itself to our bodies, and there is no turning back. A few diehard idealists are certain they can turn back the clock of time to a nobler age, but they are wrong. Technology cannot be reversed. It is a gift of knowledge and convenience that we cannot flee from. Our only hope is to learn to manage this foreigner before he completely wipes out all traces of a peaceful past culture from our minds.

Technology is not our enemy - it is most definitely a friend, an alien force that can elevate the human condition to a higher sphere of achievement and performance. Those who try to sever its tentacles do so at their own peril, for it will reproduce faster each time it is resisted. It is abounding exponentially, but it cannot become the master. It must be trained to be the servant.

It is not superior, for it is only knowledge. It is not the creator, but that which is created. Only the man and woman are made in the image and likeness of the Creator. They are called to have dominion in the earth and to subdue it. No robot race will ever outsmart their human masters, becoming self-aware and self-reproducing. Emotional consciousness, the love for beauty and creativity, the yearning for discovery and the unlocking of mystery...these are the domain of mankind alone.

Yes, unthinkable some decades ago, but now an indispensable piece of counsel for every couple who long to be happily married until parted by passing. You must master this techno-alien invasion, and vow that it will never master you.

Multitudes are, at this very moment, being mastered. Parents are failing miserably to attend to the emotional upbringing of their children. Why? Because they are enslaved by a computer gaming world of fantasy and imagination, which powerfully beckons them to escape their painful daily reality, a reality filled with the unpleasantness of dirty diapers, meal preparation, impending payments, and social obligation.

Husbands no longer have to sneak out to a darkened part of town to cater to their fleshly desires, as the darkest of worlds is opened up in a flash through the touch of a keyboard. Wives who have suffered an emotional neglect can now find empathy through innumerable electronic outlets that promise to provide someone who knows "how to listen and care." And silence has become a distant memory. We are bullied by a world of beeps, chirps, alerts, vibrations, hums, and ring tones.

Some laugh off all thought that the modern world has pitfalls, but the threat is all too real. A million plus homes are being relationally dismantled as we speak. Thousands have washed out of not only marriage, but many have even been wrenched out of the ministry. The failure to manage has opened the floodgates of an apocalyptic spirit of chaos.

And God mandates that we establish, reclaim, and hold fast to the peace and sanctity of our relationships and homes.

The rules for preserving sanity are changing as fast as new technologies are being introduced. Each new wave of advance brings a fresh demand for creative shielding techniques. But let us reach way back to the time of Jesus, and see if there are not a few timeless principles that He practiced that still might serve us well today:

- **Jesus limited the access** people had in His life. Granted, He was a <u>huge</u> people person, but even the God of perfect love established boundaries. Our marriage cannot grant 24 hour access to a world that presses in and is never satisfied. Advertisers, relatives, church friends, and media all must obey the limitations you set as the Head of your household.

- When he needed to, **Jesus disconnected**! He went off into the mountains for some quiet time with His Father. No one was allowed to follow. He preserved both His human sanity and His effectiveness by disconnecting regularly! This is the single biggest thing that 21st century couples MUST learn how to do: disconnect, at appropriate intervals, so that God, marriage, and family can be responded to without competition.

- **Jesus managed the world around Him - it never managed Him!** He was in absolute control of His own destiny, and never ran around in a frenzy or panic. He did not have high blood pressure! So learn from Jesus and slow down when necessary, take a deep breath, and reestablish control by yielding to His control and the voice of the Holy Spirit. Live a Spirit-filled and a Spirit-led life, and you will enjoy the full benefits of being a son & daughter of God!

"...a certain woman named Martha welcomed Jesus into her home, and she had a sister called Mary, who sat at Jesus' feet and heard His word. But Martha was distracted with much serving;.....Jesus said to her, 'Martha, Martha, you are worried and troubled about many things. But one thing is needed, and Mary has chosen that good part, which will not be taken away from her'." Luke 10:38,39, 40a, 41,42

WEEK #35
WHAT HAVE WE TO DO WITH TIMBUKTU?

There is an interesting Scripture that speaks of the latter part of world history, telling us that two facts will unfold: one is that "knowledge will increase," and second is that "men will go back and forth throughout the earth." (Daniel 12:4) Both of these statements have come to pass in the 21st century due to the internet and the affordable ease of air travel. We know what's out there, and we can get to even the furthest parts of it in less than 72 hours.

Simultaneous to these developments is a tendency in the USA and Europe toward Isolationism. Isolation is the concept that we should "stay out of other people's problems; we have enough troubles, economic and otherwise at home; why should we worry or get involved with every other country's headaches?"

Isolationism is very popular politically, but it is deadly to the heart of Christian religion. The parable of the Good Samaritan talks of those who passed by a man in need, until finally only a stranger (or Samaritan) bothered to change his course and get involved. It was a costly involvement, financially, emotionally, and chronologically.

But Jesus uses the story as an illustration of the heart of those who desire to be like Him. It becomes a parable illustrating what true love and true faith look like. It is a mandate for involvement in matters we would prefer not be our own. It is one of the most descriptive pictures of the nature of God.

Men pass by one another, but God, because of His driving love and compassion, cannot pass by. He sees the helplessness of mankind, man's impossible problem of sin, and directly intervenes by sending His only Son to bring the solution of the Cross and Resurrection. We are very blessed indeed that God does not believe in Isolationism.

Heaven is and was at that time a wonderful place, insulated from the problems of faraway cultures and tribes. But God determined to shed that insulation and enter into the fray. Jesus, robed in glory, "made himself nothing...becoming a servant, and took on the likeness of man." (Philippians 2)

That is serious involvement, and the polar opposite of isolation.

Married couples in days long past could be born, live, and die on the farm. They could live, bear children, and fulfill their days without ever traveling more than 40 miles away. No more. The world is thrust upon us.

If we are members of a local church, we will inevitably hear about missions, nations, short term and long term outreaches, people in poverty, hungry children and homeless mothers. We will hear the odd names of jungle outposts, languages remaining without the Bible, and tribal groups that are being reached for the first time. We will hear of wells dug, houses built, churches constructed, medical ministries, feeding centers, Christian education...and the list goes on and on. Why? Because in the words of Jesus "the poor you will have with you always."

And sometimes we simply want to live our life, turn off the TV, stop reading the headlines, and pray that it all goes away. "Why can't we just enjoy the blessings of our American way without the unwelcome interruption of miserable news reports from close to 200 countries around the planet?" Chances are God will never call us to Timbuktu anyway! (By the way, Timbuktu is in the middle of Mali, in North Africa. It was a common phrase in the Christian lingo of the 60's & 70's. You never knew when the call of God might come and send you off to some way off place like Timbuktu!")

Well, how does all this help your marriage and mine? Let us think of it in a reverse question: "How could it not help when we purpose to think more like God and align our hearts with His program for redeeming the earth?" We were not born in the 18th century. We were not born bound to the land.

We are coming to the fullness of our maturity in the days spoken of by the prophet Daniel. The nations are no longer known to God alone. We have knowledge of every land, every tribe, every people, and every tongue. And that knowledge makes us richer. Those connections bring a sense of wonder denied to previous generations, and we are privileged to live in the most potentially adventurous age of human history.

Isolationism, however, will bring all of that opportunity and privilege crashing down! Our homes will be struck with boredom, while others race around the globe joyfully manifesting the heart of God. We will bask in the security of the culture we know, while others, though stretched, are ultimately fulfilled by intertwining their lives with those who are different or peculiar.

We will stifle if we close our brains and seal our borders. How many men and women sit staring blankly into one another's faces after the children have grown and gone. There is no further stimulation. The challenge of the day is to determine that evening's TV entertainment choice. A world of wonder is at their fingertips or at the end of a jetway, but the thoughts of what could go wrong keep them home bound, comfortably apart, and purposefully partitioned.

We have one go around on this planet. I would advise all couples to make the most out of it and make every moment count. Don't just earn a living, but love living! Love this diffusion of knowledge that the 21st century avails to us. Love this freedom to see His creation, as His will and plan grant opportunity. Don't let the fear of Timbuktu, or terrorists, or tropical diseases, or even tarantulas hold you down and condemn you to an existence rather than an adventure.

Some say that we should "grow up and settle down." I say "grow up by refusing to settle for less than God's absolute best!" Don't settle for less, for average, for mediocre, for safe, or for familiar. Plunge into God's radical kingdom culture of discovery, intervention, participation, risk, faith, and fun. Thank God you tried, while others less courageous sat home analyzing. Isolationists no more, but on-the-edge-living King's kids who refuse to miss their hour of destiny. **Now** is your time!

"And the Lord said to Abram, after Lot had separated from him: "Lift your eyes now and look from the place where you are - north, south, east, and west; 'for all the land which you see, I give to you and your descendants forever'." Genesis 13:14-15

WEEK #36
SILENCE IS GOLDEN

I am somewhat embarrassed to say that I can only recall one day of total silence and solitude in my 52 year life journey. It was at the age of 16, while enrolled in a 2-week survival course for young men run by the Navigators organization in Colorado Springs, Colorado. One of our group leaders seemed to particularly enjoy torturing us to the extreme.

We were compelled to swim across a 42 degree lake, which almost resulted in the drowning of my best friend. We were denied water while on a high altitude and high temperature forced hike. It wasn't until we were at a point of extreme dehydration that they finally gave us one 8 ounce cup to share between six young guys, and we almost turned like rabid wolves on one another in our attempts to get a few sips.

I think these days such an extreme camp might be illegal. But it was a great challenge back then, and even more fun when endured with friends. Especially rewarding was the 12 mile run at a 12,000 foot altitude with the requirement of finishing in under two hours. One of my buddies made it in in 1 hour, 59 minutes, and 5 seconds, and I came in another 5 seconds later. We were jubilant! That moment 36 years ago was the crowning achievement of my athletic career, and it has been winding slowly downhill ever since!

But the greatest challenge of all during those two weeks was the test of isolation. Each of us was taken to a very remote spot near the base of Pikes Peak and left alone with our tent and water. We were to spend 24 hours without seeing another soul, then at the conclusion we were to pack up our gear and ascend solo to the summit of the 14,000" mountain.

I will never forget that 24 hours. I had never gone 24 hours without seeing another human being, and am quite sure that I have not since. It was unending. I will confess that it was not a time of complete silence, because finding the silence unbearable, I frequently initiated vocalization and muttering and even full sentences of appreciation for the flora and fauna that abounded around me.

I imagined myself the last person on earth, a daring explorer, a brave adventurer in a strange and hostile land. I also imagined that I might be devoured by coyotes or cougars or some other vile creature once darkness fell. I longed for the sun to rise so I could begin my conquest of Pikes Peak, but even more I longed to be reunited with my fellow man, rekindling my obsession with hearing others, and perhaps even with being heard.

I summited the Peak to be greeted by a lightning and snow storm, reunited with my comrades, and summarily raced down the mountain with them to avoid being struck by the lightning that flashed all around us. And I vowed to never spend a day alone again.

But I would like to break that vow. Though the busyness of life has forbid it, I've come to appreciate the power of solitude and silence. I've come to understand deeply why Jesus so frequently went off alone. Granted, I've made a number of efforts to withdraw for extended times of prayer or fasting, but these were always at hotels or conference centers. The true isolation of camping perhaps in the wilderness of a National Park or a remote desert is something I've craved, and most likely will attempt to incorporate into my future as a recurring practice.

Being happily married as I am, and enjoying tremendously every moment that I am able to be with my wife, why then would I want to retreat to that setting of 36 years ago?

What is the value of silence?

The older I become, the more I become sensitive to noise pollution. What is noise pollution? It is the incessant invasion of human conflict, the mayhem of competing media, the opinions that pour across our TV, and the advertising that assails our senses continuously. It is the background hum of electricity, the roar of engines, and the sirens that sound off as they hurry to their latest emergency. And it is often a pollution that arises out of my very own soul.

Pollution such as the need to be heard, to argue, to express my opinion (without which the world cannot navigate), or so I believe at the moment! It is my critiques and judgments of my fellow men, my pride in being right, and my anger at being thought wrong. It is my impatience with my spouse or children, my imposition of my self-perceived rights while being served, or my inflexibility when wanting my way.

There is a reason why the Scriptures speak of the wisdom of silence. Those who are wise are "slow to speak" and "quick to listen." Wisdom absorbs before reacting and forming opinions. It waits until all the information is in. It cares not if it is recognized or exalted. So much of our own noise is motivated by everything and anything except for the Spirit of Grace. We compete, complain, commiserate, condemn, and command. We find it unbearable to silently sit by when we know all the right answers.

I have sat many times with couples who compulsively correct one another in conversation. At other times I observe that one is silent, while their spouse speaks endlessly and without taking a breath. There is so often, in marriage, a perverse pollution from excessive noise.

What a delight to learn the ways of the Lord, walking together with a deep consciousness of the peace of God's presence. In times past I wondered at older couples who sat quietly eating a meal in a restaurant together. But I have since become wiser. They are not divided, not at all, but in fact have matured to a deeper place of fellowship where they've allowed one another space to reflect and enjoy the beauty of communion without commotion.

In this crazy world, silence is indeed golden. It is an opportunity to listen, to learn, and to love the heart of those who desperately need to be heard. It is more important to hear than to be heard, and this principle practiced between husband and wife brings great equilibrium and mutual respect into the home. We must allow one another space to enjoy the presence of Jesus, a greater Friend than we can ever be to one another. We must not rush to fill every void. We must listen carefully because He waits to speak in the shadow of the mountain.

"In quietness and confidence shall be your strength"; Isaiah 30:15 ;
"Be still, and know that I am God." Psalm 46:10

WEEK #37
BATTLING EBOLA IN BURUNDI

This epistle comes as we wing our way to Burundi, a tiny country in the center of East Africa. So many times in the past two weeks we've been met with a look of anxiety, skepticism, or downright disapproval as we've told folks we are off to Burundi. As it turns out, the average American knows very little about the geography of the African continent. They've only seen on the news that there is an Ebola outbreak in Guinea, Liberia, and Sierra Leone.

Now Ebola is nothing to regard lightly; it is an awful hemorrhagic fever that kills up to 90% of those afflicted. But Ebola currently is confined to West Africa, thousands of miles from where we will land. That matters not to our concerned acquaintances, because to them, **anywhere** in Africa is to be avoided these days at all costs. Burundi, Congo, Liberia or Ethiopia: to the geographically challenged, it is all the same - a fool's errand, without justification in spite of the spiritual needs of the people in these nations. "Let us stay home and out of harm's way," they say, and "as for that missionary doctor who came down with it last week...well that's his problem for being over there. What was he thinking anyway?."

I'm really not concerned about geographic illiteracy. There are greater problems revealed that deeply concern me, and should concern every Christian home. No, the problem is not the prevalence of disease, as serious as that problem may be. The

real issue that comes to light is the absolute fear that seems to grip so many followers of Christ. Ours is meant to be an overcoming faith, a triumphal procession, and a
resurrection celebration of victory over sin, sickness, and death. But we find that the realities of the new covenant have not worked their way fully into the innermost corners of our hearts.

Fear is increasing in the world today. Wars, strange and mutating viruses, and violence of every kind seem to greet us each time we tune in to the news. Yet Jesus spoke of exactly a time like today in Matthew 24 when He said "See to it that you are not troubled!"

For many, fear is Hollywood cute, optional, or accepted as a reality of this fallen world. But over and over we are commanded, not suggested, implied, or encouraged, but commanded to be without fear! When Joshua was assigned to lead God's people to inherit their promised possession, God told him "Do NOT be afraid." When Michael the angel appeared with a message for trembling Daniel, he instructed him, "Do not fear." When the disciples panicked as they saw Jesus on the water, His response was "It is I - do not be afraid." (Matthew 14:27)

The looks of horror we've received from concerned people are so transparent. They cry out "Why on earth would you go into a place of danger?." It is such a tragic question to find everywhere among the people of God. Are we not called to be heroic representatives of a risen King, marching into darkness with the power of light? Don't we know that we have an answer for every salvo fired by the enemy of our soul? Do we realize that even death has no finality over us, but is only our graduation into a condition of eternal reward and euphoria?

In economic crisis there is provision, for sickness there is healing, for natural disasters there is a promise of hope for a rebuilt future, for loss there is restoration, for theft there is recovery, for insult there is blessing, and even for persecution there is glory!

"Yea, though we walk through the valley of the shadow of death, we will fear NO evil." Why? "Because God is with us!" Is this Scripture true, and if so, how important is it to incorporate this scripture into the deepest places of our soul?

For any "believing" couple today it is VITAL. It is a non-negotiable. You MUST be a fearless family, else the list of what detains, delays, and devastates you will be without end. As long as we fear what can be taken, we are controlled.

But, when we have absolute rest in our Redeemer, His presence alone is enough and His promises are true to us in Jesus Christ. When the Divine "Yes" and "Amen" are what echoes daily through our soul - then and only then, in the face of every storm, we are fully liberated to live the abundant life of untouchable peace and joy that Jesus promised. Yet, this life seems completely out of reach for the majority.

I would encourage every couple to cultivate fearlessness. Issues of fear are real for many, and those who are bound ought not to be mocked. But let us help one another find a pathway out. Let us purpose to banish fear from our lives. If there is an area of vulnerability, tackle it in prayer. "Resist the devil, and he will flee." When dark clouds of anxiety attempt to settle upon us, let us rise up rejoicing and celebrate our kingdom culture of authority over all that runs counter to God's grace.

Let us take bold actions based on His guidance and character, and not be hamstrung by "all that might go wrong" if we dare to move forward. There are a thousand things that can go wrong on any given day, and in the midst of any given mission. But we focus instead on a thousand promises for what will go right for those who put their trust in the Lion of the tribe of Judah! "Be it unto you according to your faith!" Just make sure that it is not "becoming unto you according to your fear."

Let's teach our children to run fearlessly into a hurting world. Who wants wimpy kids anyway? Our sons and daughters must learn early on that they are children of Almighty God, royal offspring, manifesting the glory of God to a waiting world.

Here are a few quick thoughts on conquering fear (and thus equipping yourself for a full life of service and an abundant life of happiness).

1. Know God's Word and God's Promises. They are the antidote to the threats of the enemy of our soul.

2. Rejoice in the Lord always. Our praise brings God's presence, and His presence dispels the intimidation of death and darkness.

3. Recognize that the onset of fear is a "spiritual" attack first, not first a physical or emotional condition. If received, it will affect our body, mind, and emotions. But as it comes first in the spiritual realm, it must be first dealt with in the spiritual realm.

4. Meditate on God and on His Word. "He will keep in perfect peace the one whose mind is fixed upon God."

5. Find practical ways to confront fear in your life. Are you afraid of airplanes? Put up a fight and book a flight!

6. Don't be caught off guard. Determine in advance what your faith response will be should an unexpected trial suddenly present itself. Don't wait until trouble comes to frantically search for faith. Fear will always lead us down the wrong path, but faith will guide us into the wonderful security of His promised faithfulness.

Burundi, here we come!

"Therefore I remind you to stir up the gift of God which is in you through the laying on of my hands. For God has not given us a spirit of fear, but of power, and of love, and of a sound mind." *II Timothy 1:6-7*

WEEK #38
UP, UP AND AWAY IN UGANDA

As I sit high up on a hill in a suburb of Kampala, Uganda's capitol city, I am enjoying the vista of the valley below me. So much has changed in the past nine years since our first visit, and even vastly more so for the missionaries who first moved to this neighborhood 28 years ago. All around on the hilltops are mansions of varying sizes, springing up as fast as the new found prosperity (and bank credit) will allow. The neighborhood is quieter, somewhat more sophisticated, and expansion propelled by visions of a utopian future abounds.

It is not all that surprising, for 28 years ago this neighborhood was reeling with the after effects of Idi Amin's brutal repression of his nation. Witch doctors controlled the lives of the people and poverty was staggering. It was a place of darkness and fear, but into that darkness came a great light: the message of the Gospel of Jesus Christ.

And as people accepted that message, transformation came, as it always does. There is a phenomenon in mission history called "redemption and lift." Studies have shown that wherever the message of Christ's redemption has taken root and expelled the powers of darkness, there has been a corresponding increase, or "lift" in the economic indicators of that community or region where Jesus was received. Historically, economic prosperity has always followed a turning toward righteous living and Biblical ethics. As people become givers, forgivers, faithful to family, and integrity driven, the demonic curses of poverty, misery, and hunger are broken down.

But as I look around today, I see prosperity on steroids! A blessing that God intended for His people, so that they might enjoy His creation and become themselves a blessing to a needy world, has become a material obsession to out-build our neighbor, lavish ourselves with unbridled luxury, and avoid all potential discomfort in life. It is not unique to our immediate vantage point, but it is in fact a sweeping global phenomenon, as billions have internet access previously denied, and thus are able to see for themselves what they have been missing all along. Nations are in upheaval as a young generation rises up to demand what they presume has been enjoyed by the rest of the world. Everyone wants more, wants the best, and wants it for little effort or cost.

Prosperity, intended as a blessing of God, is spinning people up and away into a fantasy world of unrealistic expectations. It happened to the Israelite nation long ago. God told them of the fantastic material blessings they would inherit as they entered the Promised Land after years in Egyptian slavery.

They would have "wheat and barley, grapes and fig trees, pomegranates, olive oil and honey. There would be bread without scarcity and beautiful homes." But then God warns them not to forget where they came from, or the times when He led them in daily dependence and provision, "lest you say in your heart, 'my power and the might of my hand have gained me this wealth'." Finally He admonishes them in Deuteronomy 8:18 that "You shall remember the Lord your God,

145

for it is He who gives you power to get wealth, that He may establish His covenant which He swore to your fathers, as it is this day."

It is a Biblical certainty that God blesses and even prospers His people with an abundance. There is special grace (power) for even the attaining of wealth. But may that wealth not intoxicate us into a place where we forget the reason for the overflow.

II Corinthians 9:8 speaks of "an abundance for every good work." It says of the cheerful giver who reaps bountifully "He has spread his resources abroad, he has given to the poor; his righteousness endures forever." (quoted in II Cor. 9:9 from Psalm 112 about the blessed condition of "the man who fears the Lord").

Prosperity is needed, for without it we cannot do the work of the Lord. But prosperity's purpose must be preserved and meditated upon. Luxury and prosperity cannot become ends unto themselves. They cannot become our driving goal, for then there is no end, and our souls begin to demand more and more of the material world. Our houses are always too small, our cars too out of date. Our furniture needs updating, our clothing needs branding, and even our food must be sourced from the most organically pure stock or seed or farm on earth...regardless of the cost!

My father's heart prays the prayer of John in III John 1:2, where he declares his prayer that "you may prosper in all things and be in health, just as your soul prospers." I pray that over each of my children, and for every Christian home in every land.

Poverty is a curse, and scraping by is not the design or plan of God. Our marriages need an abundance flowing through our accounts so that we can joyfully go to the harvest fields with redemption in our message and relief in our hands. But may God deliver us from the error of excess that has shipwrecked the faith of many, who no longer dare to get down into the trenches, or experience any moment of deprivation for the sake of rescuing another. We then risk becoming a generation scarred by entitlement, self-pampering, and immediate gratification.

As husband and wife, all are well-advised to practice and anticipate God's timeless biblical principles that will bring His operational abundance into our lives. We should envision ourselves as "blessed to be a blessing."

False humility and a poverty spirit have never helped to fill anyone's belly. Governments are not the world's providers, but God's grace flowing through His faith-filled people will multiply loaves and fishes time and again. Let us see ourselves in overflow!

But as we overflow, let us then lay hold of purpose. Let us lay our treasure at His feet, praying "not our will Lord, but yours be done." Let us find our confidence and security in the faithfulness of our God, not in the glimmer of our gold. Let us remember that we are pilgrims on a journey through this world, and nothing tasted here will compare to the glories laid up for an eternity in His presence.

"...while we do not look at the things which are seen, but at the things which are not seen. For the things which are seen are temporary, but the things which are not seen are eternal."
II Corinthians 4:18

WEEK #39
THE IDOLATRY OF INTIMACY

Yes, I know. A scary title that tempts one to cease reading immediately as flashing red lights in your head are informing you that you will regret this invasive dose of marital wisdom. But fear not, things are not as they always appear. I have pledged a G-rated devotional booklet, and censorship shall not be cast away when we are so near our conclusion.

Contrary to the ascetics of ancient civilizations, we do not believe the physical senses to be our spiritual enemy. Christians have been making this error since Christendom was first began. The Bible speaks of our "flesh" as a spiritual analogy for the part of our soul that is fallen, trending always toward sin and disobedience to God.

Many take this use of the word "flesh" literally, which leads them to renounce the body and all of its sensory enjoyments. What was meant by God to become His "temple" becomes instead their greatest obstacle to freedom of the heart. They are fighting the wrong beast, for we cannot win by crucifying what God has created. The "flesh," or carnal nature of man, must indeed by crucified. Anything within us that yearns to defy the righteousness of God is our obstacle. But that which God made, our physical body with all its senses, is in itself, good. He declared it to be so, and we ought to agree with His wisdom.

But is it not true that a good thing, desired in the extreme, can soon turn into an obsession and preoccupation? Thus the blessings of taste and smell can quickly morph into a frenzy of gluttony and self-indulgence. The sensory delights of warmth from the sun, softness of fabric, the coolness of water, or the welcome of a comfy bed can quickly become our demanded experience in living, to where we no longer are available for those callings that might bring discomfort or even a moment of temporary pain.

Society has taken one of our senses and elevated it to new heights of obsession, and it is the pleasure God has given us through intimacy with our beloved. Sex and intimacy, gifts from God for the purposes of covenant, joyful physical communion, and the blessing of children, have been marketed as the highest measurement of marital success and personal gratification.

We are sold the lie that sex is everything. Some Christian counselors and authors have jumped on the bandwagon, making the attainment of maximum pleasure the quest and scientific preoccupation of every supposedly "dutiful husband and wife." The right to optimal pleasure with maximum frequency has created a generation of young men and women who quest endlessly for the partner that will measure up to the 21st century ideal of an Olympian performer as every man's or woman's right. Cease to measure up, and a search for those of greater qualification ensues.

Pleasure has become such a preoccupation in fact, that all boundary lines of what might be decent or appropriate behavior have been erased. A number of well-known marriage counselors propose that "anything and everything" is acceptable between two consenting adults. "Whatever you can imagine, go for it" is their tragic advice to those whose romance is waning. They have elevated intimacy to the place of idolatry, where the single most important factor of our marriage and happiness becomes our expertise with our partner in bed.

They are absolutely wrong, and they are corrupting the expectations and destroying the beauty of many a Christian home! Intimacy is not first about our personal satisfaction. It is an experience of giving, emotionally, spiritually, and physically. It's spiritual power lies in its selflessness. It follows the mandate of Jesus, to "consider others more highly than we consider ourselves; to do nothing out of selfish ambition or vain conceit."

Pushing the envelope of human behavior and removing all restraints off of our imagination is not what the Bible is talking about when it says that "the marriage bed is undefiled and honorable." One author takes this to mean that "any and every form of sexual behavior is legal between two married Christians." But is "determining how far we can press our boundaries" really an appropriate goal or mindset for the believer?

One must wonder - why are we even asking these questions? Do we somehow feel a moral obligation to analyze every bizarre thing concocted by the ungodly mind of a fallen world, and then study those things we can make room for in the sanctity of our homes? Is this even remotely the focus of those who are called to be disciples of Christ, light and salt in the world, holy and separated unto God, and children of the most High King?

Can we not trust, for one moment, that the precious Sprit of God, who dwells within us, is well able to lead us and guide us into a Godly enjoyment of that amazing gift of covenant intimacy. Do we really need "the world" writing our instruction manuals and gracing us with their suggestions for "10 ways to maximize this or that"... telling us how we should look, smell, seduce, and satisfy?

Let intimacy remain in its high and valued position where God has placed it in on our behalf, but let it not turn the tables of our happiness, rising up to deceive and become our God. Let us live without the pressure of conforming to some ridiculously conceived standard of biological perfection, enjoying instead the simplicity of being a couple that walk in love with God, and quite naturally then, in love with one another.

Where counsel is needed, so be it. There are times when the hidden and unresolved areas of our emotional and physical past can infringe upon our freedom to love and give ourselves wholeheartedly. But then let healing come, not by replacing timidity with hyper-virility, but by allowing the maturing Spirit of grace to flood every corner of our heart and mind. He alone can fully satisfy the heart, and the heart that has been fully satisfied by Him is freed to become all the man or woman that our spouse could ever need.

"Let a husband provide for his wife the affection due her, and in the same way the wife for her husband. For the husband and wife do not have sole authority to do as they wish with their own bodies, but each one belongs to the other. Be a blessing to one another." I Corinthians 7:3-5a

WEEK #40
DREAM ON

One of my favorite verses of Scripture tells that God takes us from "glory to glory." The Christian journey is a progression, increasing in its enjoyment as we increase correspondingly in our faith and knowledge of God.   It is never meant to become stagnant. Plateaus and reversals and long dark nights of the soul are the byproduct of our human weaknesses, but never the perfected preference of God for His children. He has designed our walk with Him so that we can forever be reaching higher and experiencing greater levels of grace.

Take all of the above and apply it to your married life. It is really true. Better days are always ahead, and the best is always still to come. Our limited imaginations cannot grasp the things God has prepared for those who love him, but freely available to you is "the mind of God," unveiled to us by our ever present Teacher, the Holy Spirit.

So in closing I challenge you to dream largely and to dream frequently. Have faith and vision and expectation for the days ahead. Recognize that your creator absolutely delights in showing off His creation to His kids. Live, Love, and Laugh; Eat, drink caffeine, and rejoice in His goodness; Enjoy the simplicity of a humble life before Him. Celebrate one another, Forgive one another, and see one another through the lens of His mercy. Love family, friends, and the fellowship of God's people.

Ours has been a journey unusually blessed and favored, for which we can take no credit. To God be the glory for the grace He has poured out. Across 90 nations we have trekked, watching His goodness proven again and again. Through the great cities of Jerusalem, Rome, Cairo, Singapore, Moscow, London and Hanoi; meandering through jungles in Myanmar, the Amazon, Borneo, Africa and India; amazed by man's handiwork in Petra, the Pyramids, and Angkor Wat; breathless to see God's glory in the mighty Cedars of Lebanon, the waterfalls of Tasmania, and the hidden treasures beneath the seas in East Timor, the Galapagos, and Curacao.

We know that no two pathways through life are identical, but I pray that the principles which have brought us profound liberation and experience will find opportunity to work their way into your hearts. Believe big and allow your loving Heavenly Father to demonstrate His goodness. And as you go forward, always remember the greatest miracles and wonders are those that He can perform within the heart, within the home, and within your covenant as husband and wife.

May your journey far exceed our own!

ABOUT THE AUTHOR

Kelly and Lenora Brake have been married since 1983, working together in Christian ministry since first meeting on an evangelism team in the lower East side of Manhattan in 1980 while students at Nyack College. The majority of each year they are active in missionary endeavors around the world, teaching and pastoring national church leaders in numerous countries. They also travel regularly across North America to share God's message with church congregations, speaking in conferences on mission or family, and encouraging people everywhere to stand strong in their faith.

For further information:

BRAKE MINISTRIES INTERNATIONAL
www.brakeministries.com
rkbrake@gmail.com
Facebook: Brake Ministries International

www.ingramcontent.com/pod-product-compliance
Lightning Source LLC
Chambersburg PA
CBHW070654290526
45790CB00001B/311